The Ole' Man 'n The Horses

Looking into the Horse's Heart

Part I of "The Ole' Man's Wisdom Series"

by

Robert J. McLardie

Published by Airé Libré Publishing & Computing Ltd.

Registered Copyright of the Trilogy:
The Ole'Man's Wisdom

Part I: *The Ole'Man 'n The Horses*
Part II: *Following The Trail - A Journal*
Part III: *His Wisdom Lives On*

Other Books by this author:
The Cornerstone Approach
The Cornerstone Approach - The Guide

BOOKS WEB-SITE URL IS:
http://www.theoldmanwisdom.com

We would like to express our heart full of thanks to:
Ministère de la Culture et de la Communication. France.
For allowing us to use the drawings of the cave horses found in Grotte Chauvet-Pont-d'Arc, in our books and web-sites.

©2005 Seven Rays Emprises Inc.
Published by Airé Libré Publishing & Computing Ltd.
Victoria BC Canada
ISBN 10: 0-9781499-0-4
ISBN 13: 978-0-9781499-0-1

© ™ 2010 "Circles of Influence" design/concept is a Trademark & a Copyright of Seven Rays Emprises Inc.

All Rights of this work are Reserved. No part or whole may be used, copied or reproduced, stored in a retrieval systems, or transmitted, in any form or by any means whatsoever, including electronic media, mechanical, photocopying, recording, or otherwise. For more information contact:
Airé Libré Publishing & Computing Ltd.
Suite 306, 185-911 Yates St. Victoria BC V8V 4Y9 Canada
Tel: 1-250-592-3099.   http://www.al.bc.ca info@al.bc.ca

This Ole`Man`s Wisdom Trilogy

is

Dedicated with Love

To

My son`s family:

Cameron

Jen

Meghan

Cassidy

The Canadian McLardie Clan

A Healing Journey

It was one of those early misty mornings, late in the fall of the year. I found myself in the pasture, walking among the horses. One old brood mare, Jay J, steps through the veil of the mist, drops into a favourite rolling spot, rolls over in both directions, gets up, and shakes the dust from her body. The fine dust particles are glinting and dancing in the rays of the early morning sun.

The mare reaches down to partake of a fresh piece of pasture, laid in abundance at her feet.

We are only some thirty feet apart. Our eyes lock, she shakes her head from side to side, exhales and walks on.

There is a moment of complete silence, during which a haunting stillness hangs in the cool morning air. I decided to sit for a while, close my eyes and contemplated on what I had just witnessed.

I stand up, stretch a little, take a few deep breaths, resolving to let go of the cares and woes of yesterday, exhale and walk on.

Horses have been a very large part of my life; they are always in the here and now. They have been my greatest teachers, have shared many gifts and insights with me, and I am eternally grateful, and thank them all.

My hope would be that within the pages of this little book, I could be the messenger of change, which our horses are waiting for, that a further benefit would be, in some small way, helping towards a change in our state of consciousness.

If you could be looking into the horse's heart, and see his soul. If you could hear him talk to you, would you listen?

This book shows you how, and it is only the beginning…

Held dear in the heart of this book is your spiritual growth, while using the guidance of the horse, as a vehicle to it.

It is not by some mere coincidence, or the game of chance, that you find yourself with this book in your hands.

Maybe you are a new horse owner, or just starting out, or maybe you have had horses for quite sometime, and yet find yourself dissatisfied, or frustrated, thinking that there is something missing in your horse relationship – or in life in general.

You must be ready for a new way.

Here is the new way – no longer a trainer, teacher or rider – but partner. This is where we are able to unite both the Human and the Horse's Spirits into a new entity.

I call it: *Oneness.*

This is when the horse would rather be with you doing things, more than anything else. Now you could be well on your way to the birth of a new relationship.

Just consider this that the lessons learned and shared with our horses could only help to enhance and deepen our understanding of Human communication skills and relationships. Riding through life, of course, is a journey. It could lead to a shift within the self, to a new awakening, to a higher level of awareness and understanding.

This ultimately, could become a change in our level of consciousness.

This is the new beginning, not only in your riding and personal growth, but also leading to the opportunity of opening the gateway to spiritual growth.

Robert J. McLardie

Chapter 1

In the desert, at the outskirts of town, a young girl just left the stables and went for a ride. She rode faster and faster until she got out of control and was thrown off the horse.

An old man was sitting on a rock, gently seeing it all. The girl was shocked, and her pride hurt. Outraged she said "This horse is no good, it's rotten, my parents should get me another one, this one is not good enough for me, it cannot do anything, and my friends laugh at me – I want a new and a better trained horse."

"Do you really, young lady," said the Ole' Man.

"Do I what," snapped the young girl.

"Want a better trained horse?"

"Yes. I do, but not this one, he is no good for anything, he has too many problems, he just wants to run, and lots of times I cannot stop him, he is a runaway."

"What if I can help you?"

"Who are you anyway, I haven't seen you around the barn or at any local horse shows, and anyway, how did you get here?" The girl couldn't see any horse or vehicle around. "I think I should get going." She stood up, but was still a little shaky on her feet and sat down in the sand again.

"Just thought you and Duke might like a little help, you know, some of those problems you just mentioned."

"How do you know my horse's name?"

"Hmm," said the Ole' Man, "seems I do know some things."

Duke had not strayed too far away; the Ole' Man asked the young girl if it was OK for him to go and say Hello to the horse, and she said "I suppose it cannot do any harm, go ahead."

The Ole' Man then, very quietly in a non-threatening manner, made a circle and approached the horse's left shoulder. He raised is right hand and smoothly stroked the horse's neck, continued to work his hand up to behind the horse's ears, and with three fingers gently started to massage this area. The reins were not broken and were hanging down. The Ole' Man continued just to talk to Duke in a quiet and reassuring soft tone, telling him he was a good boy.

Within minutes from his usual high head carriage, and at times, white and wild-eyed expression, Duke was much more relaxed, in fact his eyes were now starting to close. The Ole' Man continued to work the area behind the ears, in a few more minutes, Duke was all but asleep. His heart rate and breathing had slowed down.

The young girl had been watching and was not too sure what to think, she had never seen Duke this calm, Never!

The Ole' Man picked up the reins in his left hand, moved them gently as much as to ask Duke to wake up, and with both hands he then massaged the bit in Duke's mouth, next the Ole' Man took a deep breath and blew into Duke's nose, the horse blew back to the Ole' Man and lowered his head in response.

The Ole' Man led the gelding over to the girl. Duke walked quietly with his head and neck lowered in a calm and relaxed manner, and stopped as the Ole' Man reached the girl on the ground.

The Ole' Man, once again, asked her if she was feeling fine. After all, she had had quite a fall.

"I am just fine," said the girl, and in an irritated tone of voice continued "and just what were you doing over there with my horse?"

"Oh, not much," said the Ole' Man, "just having a visit, just talking to him and listening to him."

"Very funny," said the girl, "very funny! And just what did Duke tell you."

"Well," said the Ole' Man, "Duke told me he was willing to work on building a new relationship with you, if you were just willing to listen and feel; so what do you say, would you like to have the horse of your dreams?"

"I think you're a little crazy," said the girl.

"Well, maybe," said the Ole' Man, "but you'll never know unless you'll learn to trust and have the faith, especially in Duke. Just remember, that the horse is one of The Creator's most noble creatures, and that you are a Child of the Universe. Maybe, I am here, as a messenger, and we are all connected. We all have lessons to learn, maybe think about it on your ride back home. If you should change your mind about doing things differently with Duke, I could be available."

He stood by Duke's side, as she mounted, noticing how tensed Duke became, as she quickly took up the reins. The horse's eyes were showing a level of concern with the now obviously impatient rider.

The Ole' Man stroked Duke's neck softly saying "There's a Good Boy, relax, it's OK," and to the rider he asked that she also relax and soften the contact on the bit, and make sure her legs are not gripping his sides, because of Duke's sensitivity.

The girl seemed agitated, almost a little fearful, no doubt anxious about the anticipated ride home, the Ole' Man encouraged her to lower her hands and breathe deeply, to relax further. "Sit softly and quietly." He could have told her a lot more, but she was not ready yet. It was getting late and she had to return home.

He hoped they would be safe.

A few more strokes to Duke's neck, and he let them both go.

The Ole' Man watched for a while as they started to walk away. In no time, Duke started to jig a little and picked up a brisk trot, within another hundred yards, he twisted sideways and broke into a canter. The Ole' Man thought, such is the ride that is full of confusing and conflicting messages.

Chapter 2

Duke and the girl made it back to the barn much faster than she would have liked, but they did arrive in one piece. Duke's neck and shoulders were quite wet from sweat, and he had a white foam between his hind legs, he did look a little worse for wear after the ride of the day.

The girl quickly removed her tack and was kind enough to take a garden hose to rinse the sweat from her horse's body. He liked that, it helped cool him down. She walked him for a few minutes, put some hay in his corral and asked one of the girls in the barn to give him some water in a couple of hours, when he would be fully cooled down.

That night, in bed, the girl had many questions floating around in her head.

"Who was that silly Ole' Man, and what did he know anyway? How dare he question her knowledge, she was sixteen and had been riding from the age of five, when she had her first pony. It was that Duke had problems, yes, that was it, and Duke was a problem horse."

"She had heard some of the old trainers around the barn talk about problem horses, ones you can do nothing with, just a waste of time! Better to find another horse. She would speak to her parents, as soon as possible, what nonsense, noble creature, Child of the Universe, connected, the well trained horse of your dreams."

Yet, at the same time the image of the Ole' Man with his back to her, and Duke almost asleep then, walking towards her and stopping, as the Ole' Man stopped when he reached her, was not to be forgotten, almost haunting. Duke's neck and head were so relaxed, swaying from side to side as he walked.

Most of the time, around her, he pranced, jigged and moved around even when she tried to mount, as soon as she was in the saddle, he would trot away. Pulling on the reins, as she was often told to do, did not seem to help, although they had changed bits many times, it just seemed to make him worse.

Yes, Duke was indeed a problem horse.

"Yet again," she thought, "the Ole' Man had seemed harmless enough, quiet and even gentle, and Duke did seem to like him. Anyway, she had no idea who or where the Ole' Man came from. There was no way to contact him, all he had said was that he could be available if she changed her mind."

Well, she hadn't.

Although, she still had some unanswered questions, she fell into a troubled sleep.

She dreamed of riding in the desert, bareback with arms outstretched, even with no bridle. The horse moving under her with fluid elastic gaits, with a deeply engaged hind-end, and a floating lightness to the front-end that barely seemed to touch the earth. The horse was in self carriage performing each and every task with ease and grace. At the mere suggestion of a command, the horse would complete large and small circles, spinning and turning in every direction. Flawless halts and rein backs were achieved, tempo changes followed by powerful canter pirouettes, led to a finale of smooth lateral work on both reins.

During the troubled night, there were other parts to the dreams. Once she saw herself standing in a large open area, going to get her horse for a ride, bridle in her left hand, she sounded kisses to her horse and lifted her right hand to wave him to come to her. The horse, grazing, lifted its head, made eye contact with ears locked onto the girl and immediately started to trot over to her. He came to a graceful controlled stop just in front of her, lowered his head to accept the bridle, and willingly followed along side her shoulder. The horse stood quietly to be groomed and saddled, and when mounted, walked on quietly when requested to do so.

During the following morning, the girl was finding it difficult to relinquish her dreams, to the reality of the encroaching new day.

The horse in the dream could not possibly be Duke. Often, when she went to catch him to go riding, he would run to the far end of the corral. Even when, at times, she got close with a halter, hidden behind her back, he would swing his hind-end towards her, sometimes even lift his hind leg up, as a threatening gesture.

After considering these things, she thought maybe she should find the Ole' Man after all, what harm could it do.

The next time she went for a ride in the desert, Duke was up to his old tricks again, prancing and jigging with back hollow, his neck and head held high on a tight rein, as she hung on for dear life. The gripping made the inside of her knees sore.

It had been about a week since her first encounter with the Ole' Man. It almost seemed like a dream in itself. Was he really real? And how did he get there?

It was mid morning in the spring of the year, and yet the sun was quite high, and it was already warm.

She rode up a sand dune and as she reached up and over a rise, she thought through the shimmering haze of heat, that she could see a figure in the distance.

Duke's ears also pricked up, as he also looked to the horizon. After a few more minutes, Duke whinnied. When she got closer, she could see what appeared to be a figure bent over, moving around on the outer edge of what seemed to be a circle.

He was moving slowly. As she came up to the circle, she noticed, it was the Ole' Man. In the centre of the circle was a stick, the Ole' Man had about thirty feet of a small rope in his left hand, and another stick in his right, with which he continued to draw a line in the sand.

Duke was dancing around the edge of the fifty foot circle, the Ole' Man by now – was coiling up his soft small rope. He made his way to the centre of the circle, the circle was now complete. Up to this point, the girl and Ole' Man had not yet spoken, it was the Ole' Man who broke the silence of the desert. From within the circle, the Ole' Man said:

"Good morning, young lady, did you change your mind?"

"Well, I have been thinking about it, and I have had some dreams."

"I see," said the Ole' Man, "so how may I help you?"

"First of all, you can tell me what you are doing with this silly looking circle thing I saw you were drawing?"

"Ah well!" Said the Ole' Man, "what I can tell you is that within this circle all the knowledge of the horse world is stored, and true wisdom and learning is possible for those who dare to step over the line."

"When you do, you enter a new world, one in which, you, through the power of your mind, take control of that which causes the changes that you desire. Through faith, you learn to draw on all the resources available to you in the Universe. Within this circle you can become more aware, more understanding, intuitive, and reach a level of higher consciousness, and best of all, Duke will become the horse of your dreams!"

"All you have to do is to wake up, open your mind to change and growth, and choose to enter the circle."

Their eyes were locked and she felt touched to the depth of her soul, from which she felt the subtle rise of Hope.

Chapter 3

The mixture of the girl's dream of the perfect horse and the Ole' Man's soft spoken words had a profound affect on the girl.

Even Duke was standing still, he seemed ready! Why, because the girl was ready and more relaxed on him, because she listened to her own heart and the quiet kind words of the Ole' Man. She slid off Duke, ready to enter the circle.

The Ole' Man was now standing along side the girl and her horse, only the line in the sand separated them, each within their respective own worlds.

The girl, without knowing, reached out her hand that was holding the reins, and offered them to the Ole' Man. The Ole' Man received the reins and Duke entered the circle and stood quietly along side the Ole' Man. They somehow seemed like old friends.

The Ole' Man gently stroked Duke's neck, Duke in return, sniffed the Ole' Man's battered old jacket. The Ole' Man with a sweep of his hand gestured to the girl to enter the circle, the Circle of Knowledge and Truth. He cautioned her not to consider crossing the line in the sand, but to look up and take in the whole complete Circle of Knowledge and Truth into consideration, as entering a brave new world, because "when you choose to enter the circle and invest in your own growth, you are walking on Holy Ground."

The girl, very carefully, entered the circle.

"Well, lets not waste anymore time," said the girl. "I want to get riding, to work on Duke."

The Ole' Man then took a deep breathe, "Yes, yes, of course you do, but first I have some things I must share with you, before you ride. In fact, these messages are more important than riding, and yet, will turn your riding into a wonderful experience." He went on to say "Do you remember the horse of your dreams?"

The young girl frowned and said sharply, "Yes, but that was just a silly dream. You said you would be available, I thought you could just give me a few pointers on how to fix Duke's problems, that's why I decided to give you a chance to help me."

"Fine," said the Ole' Man, "but in order for me to offer you some help, I want you to take a few minutes and sit in the centre of the circle, close your eyes and re-visit your dream."

The girl could see no sense in this, but the Ole' Man was patient, he moved to the centre of the circle with Duke, invited the girl to sit and take a few deep breaths and relax, close her eyes, and see Duke and herself as in her dream, just as the perfect horse had been. "Just try," encouraged the Ole' Man, Duke and I'll be here for you.

The girl was reluctant at first, but having come such a long way, she decided to give it a go. After a few minutes, the Ole' Man asked the girl to slowly opened her eyes and look around the circle, when ready, just to stand up, put her hands above her head and have a gentle stretch, bring them down slowly, relax and take a deep breathe and exhale.

The Ole' Man took a few more minutes to explain that it is just so important for us to be in the right emotional frame of mind to work with our horses, because it manifests itself in our body language to the horse, which the horse reads, the moment before we even enter his space.

The Ole' Man looked off to the distant horizon; the sky was as blue as ever, with just a few small clouds hanging about. At that moment, a pleasant light breeze had chosen to pass by.

"Well, I am ready now," said the girl, "I really want to get riding Duke."

The Ole' Man changed his gaze to the ground, kicked a little sand to one side and said "I would like first to show you a couple of things with Duke, if you wouldn't mind, it will be a foundation for you to build on."

"In fact," said the Ole' Man, "no one should ride a horse until they have done this ground work with them."

The girl continued to complain about Duke's problems and not getting enough time to ride him.

"Just stay in the circle behind me and watch," said the Ole' Man, who had now taken his soft rope and attached it to Duke's bridle, by running the rope through the left side of the bit and under the jaw to the other side of the bit and tying it there.

"This acts like a soft chin strap under Duke's jaw," said the Ole' Man moving to the centre of the circle, where he started to move Duke in a small circle, the rope in his left hand was showing Duke the way, being careful never to pull too tight, which would put too much weight on Duke's left front leg and stop his front-end moving. The Ole' Man would then, with his own right leg, sweep it towards Duke's left hind leg. Duke would then step deep under his own body, crossing in front of his own right hind leg and continue to walk in a small circle in this manner, and was very focused on the Ole' Man.

After a few minutes, the rope was changed to the other side of the bit, and now with the rope in the Ole' Man's right hand, Duke performed the same task now doing a circle to the right, crossing deeply the right hind leg in front of his left hind leg. The Ole' Man and Duke's legs moving together almost like dancing.

"This is a way to exercise Duke's hind-end," said the Ole' Man, "and it will help to get him focused, before I have him go out on a larger circle. I think he is ready now to work further away from me."

At that moment the Ole' Man stepped further away from Duke and quickly positioned himself in line with Duke's hip, helping to push Duke forward to about twenty five feet away from himself. The Ole' Man seemed to come alive, quicker on his feet, more agile and fully focused on Duke, who was now trotting fairly fast on a fifty foot circle being guided by the Ole' Man's right hand through the soft rope.

The Ole' Man played with the rope, as a fly-fisherman would with a rod, reel and a light line. He would take up some slack and guide Duke with the rope using it as one would an inside rein. The moment Duke's head would give to the slightest pressure, the Ole' Man would give back by softening the pressure. It became a constant game of give and take.

Duke, being always in the moment, would quickly adjust to the Ole' Man's slightest request, the reward was instant and Duke learnt that, that was the reward. The Ole' Man had the lightest of contact with Duke, as much as possible, the weight of the rope being enough pressure to still guide and show Duke the way around the circle.

Give and take, the game went on, the two attached to each other by more than the rope, each was locked onto the other's body language. The Ole' Man at times, would take a couple of quick steps and swing the free end of the rope to cause Duke to move more forward. Duke would respond by doing a couple of faster circles with the inside eye and ear becoming more and more locked onto the Ole' Man, both becoming in tune with each other.

The reward would be when the Ole' Man would stand still, and just guide Duke as softly as possible. Duke would catch onto this quickly. The Ole' Man would also ask Duke to slow down by voice commands, always using the horse's name first, like saying 'Hello.'

The Ole' Man would say "Duke easy, there's a Good Boy, relax, relax," wanting Duke to do just that – relax, exhale and let the butterflies out, so he would realise he was safe and had a friend and a leader in the Ole' Man, someone he could trust and have the confidence in, someone who could understand him, and enter his world to communicate with him.

Duke was starting to show signs of relaxing, his head and neck were becoming lower, a couple of times his nose almost reached the ground, he had a white saliva around the bit and dripping from his mouth. Then, the moment the Ole' Man had been waiting for, Duke licked his lips, his tongue coming well out of his mouth. Next, he was chewing on the bit, and looking in towards the Ole' Man, Duke was saying "I understand, I am relaxed and would like to be with you."

The Ole' Man recognised this and in a soft tone asked Duke to come down to a walk, drawing the word out and having no eye contact, while being as quiet as possible. After a couple of requests and two more circles, Duke finally slowed down to a walk.

"Duke, Good Boy, Good Boy, Walk-on," said the Ole' Man.

The Ole' Man wanted Duke to catch his breath and fill up with air, while he continued just to walk at his own pace. A couple of times, Duke would break into a trot again for a couple of circles. The Ole' Man would ask him to walk a couple of times. When Duke did not respond, the Ole' Man would make Duke do an even faster trot, extended trot for a couple of circles. This was not what Duke really had in mind and he would glance at the Ole' Man, who seeing this, would ask Duke to walk. Duke, being a little lazy, soon caught onto the game, then walking as asked to do, quickly becoming the easier task to perform, so walk he would.

The Ole' Man was now going to teach Duke to 'Whoa' and then, 'Walk-on' as he cooled him down to finish this little lesson.

Of course, by now Duke was a little tired and using this, the Ole' Man would ask in a soft drawn out tone "Duke W-H-O-A," at the same time, the Ole' Man would guide Duke into a smaller circle around him, so as to be closer to him, the Ole' Man would then approach Duke's right shoulder to block the forward motion. Duke would stop, then the Ole' Man would drop behind Duke's hip and ask him to just Walk-on, he would let him walk on in a small circle, then again position himself blocking the horse's shoulder while lifting up his right hand as a signal, and ask Duke to Whoa.

Duke, who had been difficult to stop by using the bridle, caught onto this really quickly, he wanted to rest anyway. After doing this a few times and much praising of Duke, the Ole' Man continued just to walk along side Duke's left shoulder with the rope coiled up in his left hand.

Walking all over the circle, Duke willingly followed relaxed, head down, walking calmly by the Ole' Man's right shoulder, then the Ole' Man would just ask Duke to Whoa.

It looked like magic, Duke seemed attached to the Ole' Man. The moment the Ole' Man stopped walking, even without a verbal request Duke would simply stop by his side. To walk on, all the Ole' Man had to do was just lean his upper body forward and take a step, and Duke would walk forward. It was like they were joined at the hip; what's more, Duke would follow him all over the circle, even while the rope was fastened to the saddle.

The Ole' Man continued to make tight turns and would walk faster and then slow down, wherever he went Duke would not leave the Ole' Man's side, they were connected, they had become as one.

The Ole' Man stood directly in front of Duke, three steps away from his head, and swayed his body from side to side lifting each of his legs in turn, and Duke swayed and lifted his legs in time with the Ole' Man's, they were dancing.

The Ole' Man untied the rope from the saddle, moved in front of Duke again, and while still facing the horse, he backed away from Duke, six to eight feet away Duke tried to follow, the Ole' Man came alive and jumped forward at Duke with his arms held high in the air, landed hard on both feet and at the same time in a stern harsh tone commanded Duke "Whoa!"

Duke looked a little surprised, jumped a bit himself, but then settled and stood still watching the Ole' Man, as he continued to back away from Duke.

The Ole' Man got just about thirty feet away from Duke, before Duke could hardly stand it any longer and decided to follow, the Ole' Man as fast as lightening flicked the rope, snaking it towards Duke coming to rest under his chin. Duke looked a little surprised, but stood his ground now locked onto the Ole' Man.

The Ole' Man straightened out the rope and moved a few more steps back. He softly picked up the rope applied the slightest of pressure to the bridle, at the very same time with his right hand palm facing himself, he waved Duke to 'Come' towards him. Duke with ears and eyes now fully locked onto the Ole' Man, started to take some steps forward.

When Duke had got about half way to the Ole' Man, the Ole' Man lifted up both hands, arms outstretched towards Duke at the same time he told Duke to Whoa, Duke looked a little surprised but stopped. The Ole' Man then took up some contact with the rope, and with a wave of his hand signalled Duke to 'Come.' The Ole' Man just kept picking up the slack in the rope, as Duke continued to walk right up to him, so close he put his head on the Ole' Man's chest.

Duke and the Ole' Man looked so happy; both were more than satisfied with the progress they had made.

Duke lifted up his head and gently placed it on the Ole' Man's shoulder. The Ole' Man reached up and stroked both sides of Duke's face and then, down both sides of his neck. The Ole' Man reached into his back pocket and gave Duke two lumps of sugar.

Turning to the girl, he said "I think it is your turn, Duke should be ready to walk, and lets try to have him stop for you with no rein contact."

"Within this circle, we now have a window of opportunity to set Duke up for success and have a further good experience, for both of you, to build on," added the Ole' Man.

The whole training process had taken no longer than twenty minutes, including the time for Duke to catch his breath. Duke had blown off some steam, was relaxed, calm and warmed up, just enough time left to share something new with him.

The girl was only too glad to get back on her horse; she was very surprised at Duke's performance and had lots of questions, that could wait for a few more minutes.

"Well, up you get young lady," the Ole' Man kept the rope attached to Duke. With the Ole' Man along side, Duke stood quietly for the girl to mount.

"Leave your feet out of the stirrups and when you pick up the reins, hold them with your fingers lightly closed, just so your nails touch the palm of your hands, just take the slack out of the reins for now. You have seen Duke stop and walk on to verbal commands, so you know he can do it. Close your eyes for a moment and see him doing that while you are riding him, feel the ride, as you with a soft deep seat follow the horse's motion, with your legs hanging naturally down, lightly touching his sides – no more than that. You are to become a part of and move with the horse."

"Now open your eyes, could you see and feel that," asked the Ole' Man.

"Well, I think so," said the girl, "some of this is a bit strange to me, but I'll try to do it."

"Fine," said the Ole' Man, "Lets do it, for now I am just going to walk with Duke at his shoulder. Take in some deep breaths and breathe out any negative thoughts or tension you might have."

The girl complied and was looking much more relaxed and confident than the Ole' Man had seen her so far.

"I think we are ready to move off now," said the Ole' Man, "ready?"

"Yes," said the girl.

The Ole' Man stroked Duke's neck and up behind his ears, told him he was a good boy, he then turned his shoulders to Duke, so he was ready to lead him. The Ole' Man leaned his upper body forward and said softly "Duke Walk-on."

Duke, in anticipation of being hurt in his mouth, as his head went down to start to walk on, did raise his head and neck and looked a little concern. Much to her credit, the girl did leave the reins alone, and Duke soon felt more comfortable, softened and lowered his head, and continued to follow the Ole' Man.

To make this more solid, the Ole' Man repeated the 'Whoa' 'Walk-on' on a loose rein a number of times, until Duke did not lift his head.

"Wonderful," said the Ole' Man, "you're both doing very well indeed. Let's move on to the next part. I'll still have the rope attached to Duke, but he will be about twenty five feet away from me, we are going to do the same thing at a walk, just pick up the reins but leave the slack in them, Duke will feel the weight of the rein, and please do not pull on the reins if at all possible, agreed?"

"Agreed," said the girl smiling, starting to relax herself a little.

"Good," said the Ole' Man, "because for Duke, this exercise will help build confidence in the bridle, it is fundamental and most important."

Just as before, the Ole' Man had Duke move out on about a fifty foot circle around him, he talked to Duke in soothing quiet tones saying "Duke easy, and there's a Good Boy, relax." Duke was doing very well, saliva was starting to appear on his lips and around the bit, as he continued with a quiet relaxed walk.

The Ole' Man, from twenty five feet away, asked Duke to Whoa. The horse continued walking for another half circle and a couple of more soft requests by the Ole' Man, on the fourth request he did stop, the girl never did touch the reins.

After a few more times at this distance, Duke was really getting good at it. The Ole' Man had also told the girl that when he is to say Whoa to Duke, she should stop moving her upper body, which was moving with the motion of the horse, and think about dropping her heels into the sand and sit deep and heavy into the saddle. This was to help get the message to Duke, helping him plant his feet in the sand. The girl agreed and understood what to do. After just three tries of this method, Duke was stopping within a couple of strides of being asked to 'Whoa' without the reins moving.

"OK," said the Ole' Man taking off the rope, "I think it's time to turn both of you loose, are you ready?"

"I think so," said the girl, "what are we going to do?"

"Much the same as we just did, but you are free, you can do it," said the Ole' Man, "listen to your heart and do not forget to breath and trust in Duke."

The Ole' Man stayed in the middle of the circle, and just asked them to walk-on a large circle. The girl, only made the required adjustments with the reins to guide Duke on the circle, like the Ole' Man had done using the rope's lightest of contact.

The moment Duke was walking around quite steadily, the Ole' Man asked Duke to Whoa, at the same time the girl stopped moving her upper body and sat deeply in the saddle, with her legs just lightly against his sides. It only took a couple of times and Duke stopped. The girl smiled broadly and could hardly believe it, Duke looked pleased with himself, the Ole' Man was pleased with both of them. It was a great start to the re-training and re-conditioning of Duke, by establishing the perfect 'Whoa'.

"That was a nice Whoa," said the Ole' Man, the girl was still smiling, and Duke was standing still, quiet, relaxed, and his head held in a natural position.

"I think that's enough for Duke for today, it's important not to ask too much of Duke, we should be happy with small successes. The slow way is the fast way when teaching horses, they need time to process a new lesson and we should be careful not to confuse them, or even over work them. That way, they stay fresh and want to be with us and learn more."

"Often you'll find with horses, doing less, is doing more."

The Ole' Man left the centre of the circle and came towards Duke and the girl, offering Duke a piece of an apple as a treat. "Maybe, you could get off Duke for a few minutes and let's have a sit in the shade over there," said the Ole' Man.

Chapter 4

The girl slipped off Duke, and loosen the girth to give him a little reward. The Ole' Man and the girl, followed by Duke, walked towards the rock out cropping to find some shade to sit in.

"I am so proud of you both, you were both doing very well," said the Ole' Man.

"I would like to share with you the following; we are all a part of nature, and not separate from it in any way. Yet at times, it seems to me that as humans, we have this innate desire to try to control, even foolishly, dominate nature, instead of remembering and being humbled by the fact that we were created as a part of nature."

"I believe we should learn to live in unity and harmony with the laws of nature, and complement it to the best of our ability."

"We are of a higher order in the great design of things, but that just means that we have Free Will to make choices, which comes with more responsibility, that we should not take lightly."

"It would seem to me that at times the horse has fallen into the same category, in our eyes. Through power and control and manipulation we have tried, at times, to dominate the horse, making it subject to our will – our Ego."

"It becomes a matter of establishing a healthy balance. With regards to our horses, the natural correct approach is for us to enter the horse's world and therefore, become part of and in touch with nature at those times."

"Unfortunately, I so often find people wanting to try to humanize the horse; this can only lead to misunderstanding and confusion. The horse can always be relied upon to do what horses do best – be a horse, nothing more and nothing less."

"On the lighter side, the horse will never become a horse trainer."

"If we do not have the right approach, the result can be the so called problem horse, or at the very least, as I have witnessed, many horses that are not happy in their lives or work."

"I see them going through the motions, but look deep into their eyes, are they happy? Are they really there? Are they giving their all, really trying for their riders, being a team member? I do not think so; it should be, and can be so much more."

"Maybe you and Duke would like to work on some of these things within the Circle of Knowledge and Truth."

"Do you still think Duke is a problem horse," asked the Ole' Man.

"No, I don't think so," said the girl, "He did so well back there in the circle, I am so happy with him. I understand now that I had a couple of problems myself, sometimes it isn't just the horse, is it?"

"No," said the Ole' Man, "That's very wise of you, and that's why you are a Child of the Universe."

"That sounds funny. What does it mean," said the girl.

"It just simply means that we are all a part of so much more than we sometimes realise. All the knowledge we need is available to all those who seek it. Sometimes it's as simple as changing your mind about something, like you have about Duke."

"Yes," said the girl, "I have changed my mind."

"Good," said the Ole' Man, "That's a big step in the right direction, and there are more steps to follow."

"You did need to acquire some new knowledge and some different skills, and I helped a little with that. Now you have had a different experience with Duke, and I bet you feel differently about him."

"Yes, I do," said the girl, "I feel I can trust him a bit more now, not to run away with me, and he is more of a friend. I guess I have to take care of him too, to earn his respect."

"Great," said the Ole' Man. "That's all good stuff to build a new relationship on, and remember that's one of the things that Duke said he was willing to try if you were. I believe the two of you have made a great progress towards having a safe and fun filled riding experience. So, hold onto that thought."

The girl, in fact, had started to feel the feeling of the experience, smiled and looked over at the Ole' Man, he was bent over and she could not see his face as he looked down, speaking to the Earth. She had started to realise there was so much more to learn.

"In the next couple of days, I would like to suggest that you continue to search to become fully aware, be focused, and try your best to understand Duke fully, does that seem like something you would be interested in?"

"Yes, of course," said the girl, "But how do I do these things?"

"First, set your Intention," said the Ole' Man, "It is what matters most. Can you define what is it that you want in this relationship with Duke? You must know what you want; you must have at least a small goal, which is believable and achievable for you. A goal upon which you keep building towards, and that must become your dominant thought, each moment you work with Duke."

"Do you have a goal," asked the Ole' Man.

Her request was, "I want Duke to be my friend and that I can feel safe and be able to trust him."

"That's wonderful," said the Ole' Man. It was getting quite hot and he seemed quite tired.

"In the next couple of days," said the Ole' Man, "when you are working with Duke at the barn, to help give further depth to your relationship, I would suggest you try the following:"

"I have found that the best and fastest way to teach a horse everything and to become his friend is to do it from the ground first, which we have started with Duke. This is the time when you have the opportunity to observe your horse's every movement, each and every gait, how he moves, and length of stride, hock action and how he tracks up from behind. Is there any stiffness, is he sound and moving freely. What does his neck position and top line look like, is his back hollow or lifted up."

"Take notice of the way he carries his head. What is his facial expression, what is he saying to you with his mouth, are his lips tight and he's mad, or is there a little white foam there and he's licking his lips."

"Look at his eyes, are they white and wild staring, or are they soft, kind and blinking. Is the inside ear locked onto you as the other one scans what's happening around him occasionally. How is he breathing, check his nostrils and rib cage for signs of a rate of breathing."

"All these questions," said the Ole' Man, "give you a place to start in observing your horse. For the first time ever this may be an in-depth look at, or a greater awareness, of the whole horse. All of these physical signs are going to help you understand how Duke is doing mentally and emotionally. It will give you an awareness of his spirit."

The Ole' Man continued to describe how things will flow "More contact with the reins could be added in time, with Duke's head going down at the walk and just descending into the following supporting hands of yours, letting him know that he is to stop. The moment he has, you are to soften the contact, wait a brief moment then give the reins completely away by moving your hands forward to stroked Duke's neck as a reward."

"At times, continue to ask Duke to Walk-on just by taking up a little slack out of the reins and say 'Walk-on'. Gradually you should shorten the reins, start to feel light contact with both sides of Duke's bit in each hand. Then you would be as soft and as light as possible, as you try your best to follow the motion of Duke's head up and down."

"You are to do this all the way from your shoulders, thinking at times, that your arms are becoming so long, that you could reach a finger of each hand into the side of Duke's bit."

"You'll find yourself smiling at the level of contact and feel that you have developed. Duke would become more confident in the constant support he will receive, and would become soft and relaxed in his lower jaw. This would help relieve the tension pain and muscle discomfort he had been experiencing throughout the length of his back and loin. All of this would help to support and encourage him to move forward and freely as he had never done before."

"Gone will be the high head carriage, hollow back, stilted choppy gaits, and the jigging walk. The rough trot, in time, would become smooth, forward and fluid with ease, driven by an energised hind-end, being supported by a soft following hand. In time, all of this will come to you."

The girl was listening attentively, and realised that up to now she had had a wrong belief system that Duke was a problem horse, and without the Ole' Man's help, she would have remained trapped in the old habits, maybe for ever. The Ole' Man had told her that the mind can also be quite happy to hold on to past experiences, but they are not always what we want or need. Quite often, they are not healthy or positive, and could hinder our personal growth.

With the Ole' Man's help within the Circle of Knowledge and Truth, he had been able to help the girl receive important information, new thoughts, and to help her feel and develop new and enriching experiences with Duke.

That would help them build a new relationship and lay the foundation for a new and exciting journey together, as partners.

Chapter 5

"While you continue to work Duke from the ground and when you have assimilated all of this information, you'll be able to understand so much more about Duke as a complete horse, as an individual."

"Remember it's most important to get the basic training as correct and as solid as possible, because from there on, it is all about refining the movements to the level of excellence that you want to achieve."

"I think that's lots to keep you and Duke busy for a few days. What do you think, can you give this your best shot," inquired the Ole' Man.

"Yes," said the girl, "but I am not sure how working with Duke on a lunge line on the ground, will help us become better friends."

"Well," said the Ole' Man, "horses work with each other on the ground and communicate well with each other."

"Let me put it this way, it is because you are really trying to understand Duke as an individual, as you work with him on a lunge line in a safe area, and you are trying to motivate him to move to your signals, that he will soon start to recognise you as the leader."

"That's what horses like, to be able to follow someone. While you continue to communicate with him in this way, you'll gain his trust and confidence, and at that level of confidence, it will become mutual. You'll develop a deep and abiding respect for your horse, and become more confident."

"Horses have well-developed senses, while you work to understand Duke, he will have an opportunity to read and understand you."

"When Duke is happy and has the confidence in you, he will show respect by wanting to be with you and working for you. You'll have no problem in recognising when that breakthrough occurs."

"A horse and rider, who attain the highest level of relationship possible, can go anywhere and do anything, Take for example jumping through a large ring of fire."

"I feel we have done well today, and I do not want to overload you. When you get home, find some 3"x5" cards and write down all of the key points you can think of. May I suggest that you get to know the cards, as your own personal *Manifestation Cards*."

"What does that mean," asked the girl.

"I'll explain it some other time in more detail. For now, you can review them whenever you want. Remember to read them before each time you plan to ride Duke. It will become an empowering experience for you and Duke – more on that later," said the Ole' Man.

The girl tightened her girth and checked her tack.

"Thanks so much," said the girl, as she was mounting Duke, who only moved a couple of steps and then stood still.

"Remember to be as soft and as light with your hands and reins as possible, and keep those legs away from his sides, just keep him at a walk if you can. Have a good and safe ride home."

"When will I see you again," inquired the girl.

"I'll be around and will know when you and Duke are ready. In the meantime, just continue to work him as best you can."

"All the best and bye for now," said the ole' Man.

"Thanks again, bye for now," said the girl and with that she asked Duke to Walk-on, maintaining only a light contact with the reins. Duke was polite enough to walk on for quite a long while, the girl smiled, much progress had been achieved.

The girl recognized that Duke and herself had already started towards building that all important new relationship, the first step towards the re-training and re-conditioning of Duke. About fifty yards away from the Ole' Man, the girl stood in her stirrups and turned to wave to the Ole' Man.

He was nowhere to be seen.

On the ride back to the barn Duke was better than he had ever been. Close to the barn, Duke did start to trot, the girl remembered what the Ole' Man said, she caught herself as she started to take back the reins and she felt her legs tense on Duke's side. He reacted by raising his head and speeding up.

The girl heard the Ole' Man's voice in her head, "soften your reins, take your legs off his side, trust him." She smiled to herself, took a few deep breaths, softened contact on the bit and tried to just have her legs lightly on her horse's side.

It took a little while, as she remained calm, soft and relaxed, Duke started to do the same, the girl continued to ride along with the flow of the ride. Soon Duke found a natural place for his head and neck to be, at the same time he adjusted his trot. The girl smiled again, and did her best to just be there and to enjoy the ride, allowing her horse to flow forward and straight. After all, the barn was within sight now, and Duke knew his way home along this trail, why not, thought the girl, just leave him alone. It worked well, and Duke just settled into a nice smooth trot for the rest of the trip home.

The girl had had a long and very busy day with Duke, but was happy and content. At the barn she turned Duke out into his corral, filled up his water and gave him lots of hay, and then started her own journey for home.

Following the Ole' Man suggestion, she had found some 3"x5" cards and thought that before going to sleep that evening, she would write down some of the key points the Ole' Man had shared with her.

Actually, she made two sets one for her tack box at the barn and one to keep by her bed side, which she promised to read before going to sleep each evening. When at the barn, she would spend a few quiet moments reviewing the *Manifestation Cards*. Then while she was grooming Duke, she would consider her plan for that day's lesson with him, and she could see him performing the tasks around her at a level of excellence she was happy with. Duke would be glad to be with her, and be relaxed in his work.

The girl read over her notes one more time, they slipped from her hand as she drifted off to sleep.

The next day, the girl was up bright and early, and could hardly wait to get to the barn. The large double sliding doors were wide open, and Duke was still in his stall.

At the barn, she reviewed her *Manifestation Cards* then placed them in her tack box. She walked him to the grooming area, enjoying the sound of Duke's steel shoes coming in contact with the concrete. The sound ceased, as Duke stepped onto the black rubber mats in the centre of the alleyway where the cross ties were located.

The girl carefully attached Duke to the ropes with snaps, which formed the cross ties, and started to groom him. Starting with a strapping-blade to pull quickly some of the dirt that Duke had worked so hard to drive into his coat. Then went over him again with a stiff body-brush, and was now finishing with a soft cloth to his face.

The girl was discussing with Duke her plan for the day, and had him fully tacked up.

Over Duke's bridle the girl had fitted a halter which she could attached a lunge line to, the reins were made up safely, kept in place by the throat latch. Duke was also wearing leg wraps and overreached boots. A quick wipe down with a soft cloth to add a little shine, Duke was looking very handsome now, and ready to go to work, when all of a sudden, Duke's ears pricked forward.

At the same time, out of the corner of her eye the girl noticed something moving, coming towards them just below the bottom of the open trusses, which supported the metal roof of the barn.

Duke's eyes had become larger than she had ever seen before, and yet his feet did not move. He did not pull back and break the cross ties, which he had been known to do on several other occasions.

It all happened so quickly, the girl turned slightly away from Duke's side, looking down the main alleyway to see a Regal Hawk in full flight, sweep up between the trusses into the roof space, and land on the woodwork right above Duke's head.

The girl stroked Duke's neck and said very quietly, "Easy Duke, there's a Good Boy." She glanced up at the hawk, which was tipping its head from side to side trying to gain a better view of the pair below. It seemed hard to define who was the most surprised in this group of three.

The girl held her breath and gazed at the intruder. She could not help but be impressed by the bird's royal red streaked head, Warm brown eyes, with a vibrant yellow forehead blending into the strong black beak. Nor could she ignore the well defined strength of character to be found in the white plumage of its chest, leading down to the reddish leggings, all supported by the bird's large yellow feet.

It was a miracle that Duke, in an attempt to flee, did not blow up and pull the barn apart, in doing so he would have crushed the girl against the side of the barn wall. He hardly moved at all, just a little from side to side, to get also a better view of the hawk, perched no more than two feet directly above his head.

For the girl, the hawk stayed there for what seemed like an eternity, but it was probably only a few fleeting moments.

Without any warning, the hawk suddenly lifted up into flight, flew down to the far end of the barn, banked on its side in a tight circle, and started back towards the girl and Duke, glided above them, dipped down with wings fully outstretched to exit as quickly as it had arrived.

"Whoa Duke," said the girl, as she stroked his neck softly with the cloth, "What was that all about?"

Chapter 6

At the equestrian centre where she boarded Duke, the girl had found a small corral, it was about sixty feet square, which no one was using, the footing was sand, the whole area was a safe place in which to work Duke.

Sometimes, while working with Duke, the girl would find that she would be really focused, bonded and in complete harmony with Duke. The Ole' Man's voice would come to her, as if carried by the desert's wind.

"When I ride the horse, I am the horse."

"Think before you ride, meditate, visualise the plan, feel the ride, ride every stride, believe it and you'll achieved it."

Often it would be so clear when she was really there, really in the moment, she would look around and expect to see him leaning on the fence, only he was not there.

The girl worked Duke for the next couple of days on the lunge line, in the corral, for about twenty minutes a day. There were a few problems to start with, Duke would not want to go forward and would just turn around and face her. She remembered that the Ole' Man would make sure he would drop behind and out to the side of Duke's hip, then just by raising her arms above her head she could make herself bigger and Duke would Walk-on.

Once she got him going around her, the girl found that she could keep her place in the centre of the corral, and if needed, just swinging the loose end of the lunge line would get Duke to pay attention.

Sometimes, she started to notice that Duke would lift his shoulder and front-end slightly at the Walk-on and break into a trot. After watching this a few times she decided to make it her idea for him to trot, and then she would praise him. The girl kept him trotting for a few more circles then would ask him to come down to a walk. Duke, sometimes when asked to walk, would go faster and faster at the trot, extending really nicely.

Well, thought the girl what a beautiful trot. I am going to have you do that for five more circles.

"Duke, extended trot," the girl would say and, "go on, there's a Good Boy," and swing the end of the lunge line, she would focus on his hip causing him to continue going forward with lots of energy.

Duke carried himself nicely and even at times, arching his neck and rounding up his top line. The girl had never seen Duke move like this. Duke started to look in towards her saying I want to slow down now, she remembered what the Ole' Man had done, and had Duke just do one more circle at extended trot, before asking him to come down to normal trot, which he did.

Duke was just starting to breathe a little heavier now, but the girl decided to have him do two more circles at a normal trot and then ask him to walk. By now, Duke was a little tired and was paying full attention to the girl, he wanted to stop. The girl said to her horse "Duke w-a-l-k," he licked his lips, lowered his head and did a nice transition from a normal trot to a walk.

The girl decided then to have Duke walk for a couple of circles, "Walk-on Duke," she said. Duke was willing to walk. It had taken only a few minutes to work through an extended trot, to a normal trot, to a walk; it was also good conditioning for Duke.

This way, he could practice the transition on his own, free to move without a rider being in the way at all. He had a chance to learn by himself and at the same time becoming fitter and have the opportunity to improve his overall condition, which would eventually help him to carry his rider.

The girl's plan was to work Duke equally in both directions and she had started Duke by going on the left rein, circling to the left in a counter-clockwise direction. She then asked Duke to Whoa, coiled up the lunge line and walked up to Duke's to praise him, "Good Boy Duke, what a smart boy."

The girl stroked his neck, and stood there quietly with him while he caught his breath. The girl then went on to work Duke to the right, she found that he was a little harder to get going this way, but she was determined, Duke seemed to pick up on this, and after a few attempts she had him going to the right.

The girl could soon see that Duke was stiff going this way, he was not as fluid as going the other way, it seemed to make sense to her to work Duke a little bit more on his stiff side, and she made a mental note to herself that the next day she would start Duke on his right side first, just to help him become equally flexible on both sides.

At the moment, the girl was able to get Duke going to the right, he seemed a little concern and overexcited. He was not used to doing so much to the right and was feeling uncomfortable about it, he wanted to stop and turnaround to go left.

The girl stayed calm and relaxed, took some deep breaths, following the Ole' Man's instructions.

It took her three or four tries, but eventually Duke was going right, although not so happy, and going quite fast at an extended trot. Well, at least he is going right thought the girl, I'll make the best of it and have him continue this extended trot.

"Duke, extended trot," The girl thought she saw Duke almost frowned and his lips became tight, his eye was staring, he looked a little mad.

"Good Boy Duke," said the girl, "Good Boy go on." If he's mad, thought the girl, that is his problem. The girl stayed in the centre, after two or three fast circles, Duke started to get himself together.

His eyes were blinking now and his lips not quite so tight, he was starting to relax. The girl continued to keep Duke at an extended trot until he started to show signs of wanting to slow down, she asked him then for two more circles, therefore, making the extended trot her idea and that Duke was doing it, because she was asking him to do so.

Then the girl said to Duke, "Duke extended trot." Of course, Duke by now wanted to slow down, he had used quite a bit of energy running around. Again, the girl used this to her advantage by motivating her horse to do one or two more circles at extended trot by being disciplined and determined herself, and then asking for the normal trot.

At this time, both horse and girl wanted the normal trot, it became a win-win situation. This way, the girl was placed in the position of a leader in this little herd, by causing things to happen. The girl was pushing for two more circles, keeping the horse moving forward, the horse responded to this; the result was that the girl gained the horse's respect. Trust and confidence in each other can be built when you have this level of respect.

The girl worked Duke in this manner for the next three days. After each lunging session, she would ride him lightly in the large outdoor riding ring, as a way to cool him down. It would be just a casual ride around, nothing too demanding, sitting quietly with a soft following seat.

She went on a ride down the driveway and headed out along a favourite desert trail. She made a point to ride Duke on the lightest of contact to help re-establish his confidence in the bridle; her legs would be lightly placed on his sides.

She did not go too far from the barn on these small trail rides, it was a nice relaxing way for them both to finish the day. Duke continued to respond nicely, this would be the way.

On some occasions, as she would ride out to the desert, the girl would hear the Ole' Man's voice again, as soft as a breeze:

"As Duke right-hind comes forward," he was whispering to her, "and while following with your soft deep seat, allow your right hip and leg to become one with his, and flow and walk forward with him. You do this with each stride Duke takes, you join in the walk with him, it's passive yet supporting, you learn not to get in the way, but feel were his hind legs are with each stride."

"You flow, he flows."

The fourth day was a day of rest for Duke, he had worked very well.

On the fifth day the girl was surprised that Duke was willing to go to work. It was like he had had time to process the things he had been taught. He was happy to see the girl. In the corral she continued with the same consistent training program. She gave the same body signals asked him always by name to perform the required gaits. Worked him in both directions, gave him lots of time to get his breath back and relax, and made sure to find the right time to praise him a lot.

It had been six days since the girl had first met the Ole' Man in the desert and time again to give Duke a well-deserved day off. The girl did go to the barn to see him, he was laying down sleeping in the afternoon sun, she walked into the corral, lightly brushed him and gave him an apple.

"I think it's time to return to find the Ole' Man," the girl whispered to Duke, we will go tomorrow, are you ready, because I am, and I think there is a lot more to learn for the both of us. Duke watched her walk away.

Early the next day the girl was at the barn; Duke had finished his morning feed and was in his corral. The girl brushed and tacked Duke up, took him to the small corral, and put him through the same routine she had been doing during the last seven days or so.

Duke went very well, just as the girl expected him to. She smiled, really liking the way Duke was stopping now to the word Whoa. After about twenty minutes of lunging him, the girl rode down the driveway and out into the desert to find the Ole' Man.

Chapter 7

The girl circled a few trees on her way; it gave Duke something to do and focus on. There were some trees that were close together, and the girl did a few figure eight patterns in both directions, then continued on her way.

A couple of times she felt confident enough to ask Duke for a normal trot, most of the time it went well, sometimes he would speed up, the girl did her best to remain relaxed and trust him, keeping light contact with the bit and not pulling back in fear, made a huge difference. The lunging work in the corral seemed to be well worth it.

Duke and the girl relaxed into the ride. She had so many questions for the Ole' Man, she could hardly wait to find him.

After about another hour of walk and normal trot in the desert, the girl could see rising out of the desert the large rock out cropping of numerous shades of browns and reds changing all the time, as the sun banished the shadows from the ever-changing face of the rock.

Something seemed to move in the deeper shadows to the east of the rock base. She could see the Ole' Man walking slowly, a little bent over, finding his way to a comfortable place to sit in the shade.

The girl smiled, Duke was trotting, and in the excitement of the moment, almost without realising it, the girl had tensed both of her legs. Duke responded by extending his trot, the girl left him alone, as they both continued towards the Ole' Man.

When the girl reached closer to the rock out cropping, she had room to make a very large circle at the extended trot. It worked well to steady Duke. On the second time around she asked him for a normal trot, Duke complied. The next time she passed close to where the Ole' Man was sitting she asked Duke to walk, it took another half circle before Duke came calmly down to a walk. The girl walked the remainder of the circle and up to the Ole' Man.

"Well my," said the Ole' Man, "is this the same horse," as he walked over to stroke Duke's neck, "what a Good Boy Duke, what a smart boy you are."

"And you young lady, I am so proud of you, you have changed to become a thinking and feeling rider."

"Come, give Duke a break, sit over here and tell me what the two of you have been doing."

The girl dismounted and the three of them found a shady area to relax in.

She quickly recounted the events of the last number of days. Using a small and safe corral and the lunge line to help keep Duke focused on her, how each time before asking Duke to work, she would prepare herself mentally and have a plan for their lesson, visualising the end results she wanted from Duke even before starting to work with him.

"You and Duke are doing very well," said the Ole' Man, "I am pleased with both you. By the way, Does Duke happen to like apples?"

"Oh yes," said the girl, "It's his favourite treat."

"That's good news," said the Ole' Man, "because I just happen to have a couple with me, I would like to show you and Duke how to play this little game, which will also increase his learning curve. Can we get started?"

"Yes," said the girl, "I'm ready."

They all entered the Ole' Man's world within the Circle of Knowledge and Truth once more.

The Ole' Man attached his rope to Duke's bridle fastening to the left side of the bit, so he could work Duke going to the right rein, clockwise. He started Duke on a small circle and gradually had him go further away from him until Duke was about twenty five feet from the Ole' Man, and was now standing still in the centre of the circle, and only turned on the spot as he followed Duke's movement.

The Ole' Man had Duke going at a nice extended trot then, asked him to do a normal trot for couple of circles, Duke was relaxed and working well. The Ole' Man praised the girl again for the fine work she had been doing.

The Ole' Man asked Duke to walk; Duke took about another half a circle and then came down to a nice quiet walk. The Ole' Man praised him "Good Boy Duke, Walk-on, go right." One More Circle and he asked Duke to Whoa.

"Duke W-h-o-a," the Ole' Man said in the now familiar soft drawn out tone, Duke stopped and looked in towards the Ole' Man. The Ole' Man gathered up his rope as he walked towards Duke, "Good Boy Duke," and stroking his neck said "what a smart boy."

The Ole' Man said that today, at this level of training, Duke was really doing well, and it was important to recognise that and accept it, and always to reward him for trying.

He took a knife and the apple from his pocket and cut it into small pieces, and gave a piece to Duke. The rest he put back into his pocket. "I am going to help speed up the learning process, and test just how obedient he is, and try for a quicker response when we ask him to do some task. To start with, I'm just going to have Duke walk a circle; about fifteen feet out from me and then ask him to Whoa.

"I'll get started," he said to the girl.

The Ole' Man soon had Duke going in a nice relaxed walk. "I am going to asked Duke to stop in the same place every time, right by that large rock over there on the edge of the circle," said the Ole' Man, "so he gets used to doing it by repetition in the same place, then I'll give him a treat sometimes, you'll see how it goes."

"I know Duke can do this," added the Ole' Man.

While Duke started to get close to the rock, the Ole' Man said "Duke Whoa," he did this two or three times. On Duke's fourth try he was really close by the rock, the Ole' Man praised him and said "Good Boy Duke, Good Boy," gathered up the rope and walked up to Duke with a piece of the apple in his hand, and gave it to him.

Duke liked this game, because the next time around he was only too willing to stop. You could actually see him starting to slow down, really paying attention – trying harder, but to make sure he would understand that he was to stop only when the Ole' Man asked him to, the Ole' Man would say "No Duke, Walk-on," and made sure Duke paid attention.

The next time around, the Ole' Man gave Duke lots of time to get ready and then asked him to Whoa. Duke stopped very close to the rock, the Ole' Man rewarded him with another piece of apple and lots of praise.

Duke was really paying attention, "I am sure he will stop right by the rock this time, you wait and see," said the Ole' Man to the girl, "just watch and focus all your attention on Duke's shoulder stopping exactly in line with that rock – ready?"

"Yes," said the girl, "I am ready."

"Pay close attention to the whole horse, watch every stride."

"Duke Walk-on."

Duke glanced at the Ole' Man as if to say "OK, I understand, let's get on with it."

Duke picked up a nice even walk, the closer he got to the rock the more you could notice his inside ear was really locked onto the Ole' Man and his eyes were blinking.

About three horse lengths away from the rock, the Ole' Man said "Duke," hearing his name Duke actually, while still walking slightly turned his head in towards the Ole' Man.

Duke was now ten feet away from the rock.

The Ole' Man said "Duke Whoa," as Duke took his last step; his shoulder came in line with the rock. "Good Boy Duke, Good Boy," said the

Ole' Man, quickly coiling up his rope and approaching Duke.

Duke was all eyes and ears on the Ole' Man, but his feet did not move.

Duke was soon into his second piece of apple, looking very pleased with himself, and the Ole' Man and the girl were both stroking and praising him.

"As you could see," said the Ole' Man, "Duke was set up for success, and he is learning.

"We are presenting to him learning opportunities, with intermittent treats, the apple, or stroking and verbal praise. I think you'll agree, that Duke responded by being more focused and trying harder."

"We are motivating him, teaching him," stressed the Ole' Man.

"It is also very important to realise that we have to be very focused and right here with Duke, fully aware, paying attention to every little movement or signal that Duke give us, so we can understand what's happening with each and every moment in Duke's world, while we are working with him."

"I am now going to have Duke work at an extended trot to warm him up, then I am going to have him do two circles at a normal trot and then, I'll ask Duke to stop right where he's standing now," said the Ole' Man.

"That's my plan and I believe Duke can do that, what do you believe," he asked the girl.

"I believe he can," said the girl, who was happy indeed with all she had seen Duke do in the last few minutes. She stroked Duke's neck, "Good Boy Duke, you are so smart."

"Continue to stay focused and watch Duke intently," said the Ole' Man to the girl.

The Ole' Man soon had Duke moving very freely forward doing a beautiful extended trot for three or four circles. You could see his inside eye was on the Ole' Man, and his inside ear flicked backwards and sideways towards the Ole' Man, who continued to talk to Duke in soft tones,

"Duke extended trot, go right," always reassuring Duke, "there's a Good Boy, go on, go right, relax."

The Ole' Man would always use the same simple consistent language as commands to give Duke the required instructions, and always would give some form of praise for the slightest try by Duke. This was the key to success in training Duke.

It was also his promise not to confuse Duke.

"Duke normal trot, normal trot," Duke adjusted to a normal trot, "Good Boy."

Giving instructions to the girl, the Ole' Man said "watch Duke, stay focused two more circles at this normal trot and then the big finish by the rock, become fully aware of how Duke is moving, take in as much as you can about his complete body language, be in the moment with him, stride by stride, it's most important.

"Remind me to explain it later," said the Ole' Man.

Duke had completed one full circle and was doing very well, relaxed in body and mind. He had just passed the rock and the Ole' Man started to talk to him to reassure him.

"There's a Good Boy, go on, normal trot, go right, relax."

About thirty feet from the rock the Ole' Man said "Duke," at twenty feet, "Duke Whoa."

Duke overshot the rock by about ten or twelve feet.

The Ole' Man quickly rewarded the try by saying "Duke, Good Boy," but straightaway he asked Duke to Walk-on. Duke looked a little surprised but did walk on, the Ole' Man quickly moved Duke up through normal trot to extended trot within a couple of circles.

He then asked Duke to do a normal trot, to get him settled and fully focused within a couple of circles.

"Good Boy Duke, Good Boy, go on, go right, normal trot," the Ole' Man was more intense and Duke responded, by being focused, paying attention, in tune with the Ole' Man.

"Focus on the rock and see a beautiful stop, feel it," said the Ole' Man to the girl.

"Duke, Duke," said the Ole' Man a couple of times to help refocus the horse.

Again at thirty feet away, "Duke, Good Boy."

Twenty feet away, "Duke Whoa," and then again a drawn-out "W-h-o-a."

Duke came down from his normal trot, did a few strides at walk, and stopped just before the rock.

"Good Boy, Good Boy," said the Ole' Man and the girl together.

Duke looked in towards the Ole' Man, as if to say "hurry up, where's my treat."

The Ole' Man looked quite happy, as he walked over to Duke with a treat in hand.

The girl was there first, stroking his neck and body, and saying, "Good Boy Duke, Good Boy, what a smart boy you are."

The Ole' Man gave Duke another piece of apple, "there's a Good Boy Duke well done," said the Ole' Man.

"I am very pleased with Duke," said the Ole' Man, "he is very kind, he really tries, you cannot ask for more than that."

"Let's give him a well-deserved break," said the Ole' Man, "he's done so well."

"Yes, I think so," said the girl, "I am so happy with him."

"He really can learn well when lessons are presented to him step by step, in a simple way he can understand," added the Ole' Man.

"You asked me to remind you about something, I think it was about me paying attention to how Duke was working. What would that be all about," asked the girl.

The Ole' Man was still stroking Duke smiling broadly enjoying the moment.

"Yes, yes of course," said the Ole' Man. "I wanted to pass along to you something that I think is so important to realise. When we spend time trying to teach our horses various things, we try to enter the horse's world, and as we just worked with Duke within this circle, we have a unique opportunity to observe him."

"It will take you a fair amount of time and effort to be able to take all of this in, but Duke, given a chance, will become your greatest teacher. You just have to search to become fully aware, be focused, and try your best fully to understand Duke for whom he is."

"Always remember to be calm, relaxed and yet positively assertive, try to set him up for success and always praise him at every chance you get. Then give him time to take a break and catch his breath, never running him out of air."

"Remember to be good and kind to yourself," said the Ole' Man.

"There is no such a thing as a failure; you always produce some kind of result. Be prepared to accept today, in this moment, the small improvements Duke gives you, he will always be trying. Search in your heart for what went right and learn to move on. Always build on positive results and keep doing. Continue to make adjustments until you achieve the desired results."

"So what do you think so far, is this being of any help for you and Duke? Do you think you can continue to work Duke by yourself," inquired the Ole' Man.

"I am so pleased with Duke right now, but I know there is such a lot more to learn. You said you would be available, and I am on my spring break from school, I was hoping you would give me some more ideas, so I could continue to work with Duke."

"I know he is stopping when I stay Whoa, I'll need to have more contact to teach him to do other movements, even if it's only a light contact, so I would like to know how you would do that," said the girl.

"I would also like, of course, to ride him in a collected frame. Now when he stops – it's fine, but he is all stretched out with his nose sticking way out in front," added the girl.

"Of course I'll help," said the Ole' Man, "you'll have to promise to do most of the work, and I am sure Duke will do his part."

"So you'll help me," said the young girl.

"Yes," said the Ole' Man, "and I think we had better get started before it gets too hot."

"Let's enter the Circle of Knowledge and Truth," said the Ole' Man. The three of them entered the circle, back into the Ole' Man's world.

Since Duke had been standing around for a while, the Ole' Man fastened his rope to the bridle, and put Duke through transitions adding canter, so he could have Duke do canter to trot, trot to canter and down to a walk. Only for a few minutes each way, just to have Duke become re-focused.

The Ole' Man told the girl that he was most impressed with the progress that Duke had made, and it was now the time to increase the degree of difficulty for him. "I am going to slowly introduced Duke to understand the acceptance of light contact on his bit by using what is called Side Reins," said the Ole' Man.

"I have made my own with soft elastic, that only requires two pounds of pressure to stretch them. I have found, that using this method allows the horse to help teach themselves about light pressure and release, or as we say to the rider 'soften the contact.' I am quite sure this soft elastic is far more giving than most people's hands are, when they are trying to teach their horse what to do while riding."

"Let me show you." With that the Ole' Man reached into the jacket pocket and brought out his Side Reins with buckles on them for adjustments.

He attached the Side Reins to Duke's bit and to the saddle, and to start with – they were absolutely loose. The Ole' Man now had Duke do a couple of circles each way, he then had Duke Whoa, then he walked over to Duke and praised him.

With his hand on Duke's nose, he applied some light pressure, Duke resisted a little then softened and moved his head away from the Ole' Man's hand, "Good Boy," said the Ole' Man.

Then with the Side Reins in each hand, the Ole' Man set about lightly massaging Duke's mouth with the bit, Duke again, at first resisted, but quickly softened.

The Ole' Man placed his left hand on Duke's nose again with some light pressure, Duke softened quickly, the right hand shortened the left-side rein, he quickly put his right hand on Duke's nose and adjusted the right-side rein.

All this was done in order to ask Duke to bring his nose two inches in from where it had been, poking way out in front.

The Ole' Man stayed close to Duke and walked him round for a few minutes, to let him start to feel some of the slight contact at this level, so as not to scare him, and upset his confidence.

Duke was walking calmly and doing very well.

"See," said the Ole' Man, "so far so good, it's so important to set him up for success, and have a good experience to start to build from."

"Just look, Duke is testing the Side Reins, as he walks with me, pushing his nose out after a couple of strides, he would soften on the bit bringing his head in a little."

"I think he is ready to go to work on the circle, I'll have him walk and then trot a little, and then back to a walk and then, Whoa a few times, so he can continue to develop a feel for the contact."

"I want you really to pay attention to the horse's complete top line and of course, keep glancing at his head and mouth especially during the transitions," the Ole' Man stressed.

"Our little goal is to have Duke just carry the bit and have slack, or very light tension on the Side Reins."

"When he starts to work, you are going to see him push into the bit, as he would if you were riding him. I believe and expect that Duke is smart enough, that after a couple of tries he will soon decide to carry his head in a little different position."

"Then he will learn to maintain it during the up and down transitions, let's get started and give Duke a chance to show us how smart he is." With that, the Ole' Man had Duke walk-on, doing a large circle. He could see by the expression on Duke's face that something was different and his lips did look a little tight and his mouth was dry.

While Duke walked he would at times, because his head would go up and down, push into the bit and easily stretched the soft Side Reins, he would move his head from side to side, as if to say 'what's this'.

The Ole' Man asked Duke to trot, and now the head became steady during the two beat diagonal gait, but of course Duke was used to being able to poke his nose straight out ahead, now he was required to have just a slight bend from poll, just by bringing his nose in two inches. Duke fussed a little, but not too much, because the change was in fact small.

After a couple of more circles at normal trot, the Ole' Man asked Duke to come down to a walk. "Watch now," said the Ole' Man, "watch Duke's head," Duke handled the down transitions quite well, he pushed at the bit a couple of times, as he tried to adjust to the up and down motion of his head, within half a circle he had found a place to carry his head on a light supporting rein.

"There's a Good Boy," said the Ole' Man to Duke, and then, "Duke Whoa." Duke was happy to Whoa, and the Ole' Man gathering up his rope, walked over to Duke and started to praise him and stroke him and invited the girl to come over and do the same.

"Why don't we give Duke a little break to catch his breath and relax, and process what was happening," the Ole' Man really just wanted to discuss some information with the girl.

"What a Good Boy," said the girl.

"Yes," said the Ole' Man, "I want to explain something to you, before we go on and start the next process."

"Have you ever had the opportunity to see Duke running free, really using himself, what I might call being animated?"

"Yes," said the girl, "not long ago, a new mare came to stay at the barn. She was put in a corral next to Duke. He trotted up and down the fence line showing off, I would say actually, so did the mare."

Duke arched his neck, his back seemed to lift up, and he really bent his hocks. At times he would just burst forward with lots of energy."

"Great," said the Ole' Man, "do you just happen to recall how his head was positioned?"

"Yes," said the girl, "I do, it was almost vertical, at times his front feet barely seemed to touch the ground, as he extended his trot, he seemed to be floating across the ground."

"That's just the type of carriage we are going to train Duke to do when you ride him, does it sound interesting," said the Ole' Man.

"Very," said the girl, "can he do that?"

"Of course," said the Ole' Man, "let's get started and give Duke a chance to show us his stuff."

"Look for moments of it, as Duke works, even just a stride or two, you'll have really to concentrate, to be there, every moment. Are you ready," said the Ole' Man.

"Yes," said the girl, "I'll do my best to be focused."

"Great, then Duke and I'll begin," said the Ole' Man.

"Watch again the head and later Duke's hock action, as I ask him to go from the walk to a normal trot a couple of circles, and then extended trot," said the Ole' Man.

"One of the main reasons to do this is to have Duke bend, or engage his hocks and to drive forward. That will encourage him to lower his croup. What we need to understand is that right from behind his ears to the top of his tail, all those muscles are interconnected, so when he is moving like that, driving from the hind-end, he will actually lift up his abdomen and round that top line. That in itself is what really truly brings the head closer and closer to that vertical position that most of us are trying to achieve, while riding our horses."

"It goes without saying, that you must not forget to work Duke through the transitions in both directions," said the Ole' Man.

Duke continued to fuss a little with the bit, as can be expected at this level of training.

After three or four circles at extended trot, Duke was already starting to get more comfortable with the bit and the light contact through the Side Reins. The Ole' Man would then ask the horse, "Duke, normal trot," so Duke would adjust his stride at the same time as adjusting his head set accordingly. "When doing extended trot, can you see how when Duke steps deep underneath himself, that he bends his hocks more to step forward, and that he lowers right from the croup area."

"You might think that the Side Reins are bringing his head closer to the more vertical frame, that's what most people do like to see and refer to, as being collected or working towards self carriage."

"Its not the elastic Side Reins that produce the desired result. It's the driving from the hind-end of the horse, through his body and into the bridle. The bit is only there to receive that energy and give the horse direction through the rider's following and supportive hand," explained the Ole' Man.

"When I asked Duke to lengthen and shorten his stride through extended and normal trot, I am helping Duke exercise all those muscles from his ears to his tail. It's Duke actually lifting up his abdomen that helps produce the rounded top line that we see."

"It's a natural extension of all those things, that also helps Duke's head become closer and closer to the vertical. While the horse becomes gradually more and more conditioned and therefore stronger, he actually compresses himself more and more. The effect is the more rounded top line, which is much stronger and therefore, he is more able to carry the rider."

"Being stronger in the hind-end also means that he learns to carry more weight back towards the hind-end, Duke's centre of gravity will actually move more towards the rear. This helps lighten the front-end, now the front feet are more freed up to do what it is that Duke needs to be doing with them."

"His front feet will not be getting in the way of his forward movement," as the Ole' Man was describing all of these things, he was still continuing to work Duke in the circle.

The Ole' Man really had Duke going nicely, doing up and down transitions, normal trot to extended trot, and extended trot back to normal trot.

"This is hard work for Duke," said the Ole' Man, "I am going to have

Duke just walk for a while, so he can relax and catch his breath and I'll have him stop by the rock and give him a piece of apple, as a treat."

Duke made a beautiful transition to the walk and walked for a couple of circles on a light rein very relax, saliva was dripping out of his mouth.

Duke had time to recover fully from his trot sessions, and so the Ole' Man brought Duke into the centre of the circle to give him a further chance to relax. He stroked him, "Good Boy Duke," and they were joined there by the girl, the Ole' Man then removed the Side Reins and continued to stroke Duke and gave him a couple of pieces of apple as a treat.

"Before we continue working on the next session with Duke at canter, I would like to say that I am so pleased with the way that Duke is working," said the Ole' Man. "I just want to work him through trot to canter, and then canter back down to trot, this is a great conditioning exercise. One of the main benefits is that the horse has to change from the three-beat gait of canter, to the two-beat diagonal beat of normal trot."

Duke will have to learn to balance his head and neck as he changes stride and hock action, when he learns to do this, he will have a chance to develop the feel for and experienced the contact of the bit through the giving supporting soft and flexible Side Reins, which will be fine for now, at this level of conditioning and training. Remember, it's most important for us to help develop the horse from his hind-end, that's the key."

"We must never lose sight of that," added the Ole' Man.

"The Side Reins, for now, are only being used to help Duke recognise and learn to accept a certain level of contact, pressure on the bit, which can be measured in pounds per square inch. While he continues primarily to drive forward with continuous free flowing movements, which working on the circle helps us to produce."

"For now, it's a great benefit for Duke not to have to worry about a rider, whose hands might not be all that forgiving, as the Side Reins are," the Ole' Man went on to explain.

"At this level of training, Duke has enough to learn without anyone hurting his mouth, which of course would have the effect of causing the horse not to want to go forward, and this causes all kinds of problems."

"I would like you to understand that this is a part of a progressive innovative training programme. The first priority is to help the horse to learn how to do many things at liberty, like free forward movement, developing his gaits and transitions, before he is even being ridden."

"Getting the horse fit and conditioned mentally and physically is of the utmost importance and again, before we place demands on the horse as riders, but which the horse is not physically qualified to do, this causes him pain, confusion and it is just not acceptable, then we often say that he is a problem horse, but we taught him to do what he is doing."

"I think that's enough talking from me, even Duke looks a little bored with me rambling on. Let's have him do some of the canter and trot work."

"I would like you to pay attention, as I put Duke through these transitions, pay particular attention to how he adjusts his head, which will be the extension of what he's doing with his hind legs and through his top line. That means right through the hind-end, the loin, his back, up to his neck and then finally his head."

The Ole' Man re-connected the Side Reins, "there's a Good Boy," he said while stroking Duke's neck and shoulders. The Ole' Man then went about refocusing and warming Duke up by starting at the walk for a few minutes, then he had Duke pickup a normal trot.

He continued with this until Duke became relaxed, then he asked for a couple of circles at extended trot. Duke was now exhibiting free flowing strides and was focused on the Ole' Man.

The Ole' Man said to the girl, "You see each time we work him he just gets better, more confident in his own ability to perform these gaits and transitions.

"Yes," said the girl. "I would say that he looks happy and relaxed doing it, even enjoying himself."

"Good," said the Ole' Man. "I agree, and that's how I like to see horses working. I am going to have Duke complete one more circle at this extended trot, then when he gets to the walk I am going to ask him to canter."

"Of course I'll give him lots of time as I prepare him in three stages." The Ole' Man then went on to explain, "as usual I'll call his name, Duke canter, in two well-defined syllables and I'll slap the loose end of my rope on my leg to make a noise, if when you are working at the barn and you have a lunge whip, just snap it in time – in the last part of canter."

"I find that a little noise like this is of benefit to make, in the early stages of training to the canter depart, remember Duke has cantered before, but not with the Side Reins on."

On his first try, Duke was well past the rock before he started to canter and he was a little unbalanced, and this being the first time cantering with Side Reins, he did fuss with his head and neck, as was to be expected. The Ole' Man was quick to praise Duke the moment he picked up the canter, "Good Boy Duke, go on, canter, Good Boy, easy, relax."

The Ole' Man used lots of praise in a soft reassuring tone while he supported Duke around the next couple of circles. When Duke approached the rock again, the Ole' Man asked Duke to come down to an extended trot, very close to the rock. Duke willingly completed the down transition to a steady extended trot, to which he received lots of praise from the Ole' Man, who was very focused on Duke and encourage Duke to go on, and do a couple of more circles. Using the rock again, the Ole' Man asked the horse, "Duke normal trot."

Duke was a little tired at this point and really seemed to catch on to being asked at a consistent point – the rock, by consistent verbal requests, being easy to learn. Duke proved this by coming down to the normal trot right by the rock, "Good Boy Duke," said the Ole' Man.

The horse started on one more circle towards the rock, "Duke, Duke," the Ole' Man called out to get his attention, "Good Boy, easy."

Then, "Duke walk," Duke's right front foot landed right alongside the rock at the walk, "Good Boy Duke, Walk-on," the Ole' Man wanted Duke to complete the circle.

About twenty feet to go to the rock, the Ole' Man was very focused and called out to Duke "Whoa," it was amazing, Duke's shoulder just hid the view of the rock from the Ole' Man. "Good Boy Duke," said the Ole' Man as he coiled up his rope while heading towards Duke, he reached Duke and removed the Side Reins. He reached into his back pocket and took a small piece of apple as a treat. The girl joined the Ole' Man and both of them continued to stroke Duke and give him lots of verbal praise.

Even though Duke, during the sessions, had worked quite hard and was sweaty and a little tired, it was plain to see that the horse seemed happy with his own performance, and he loved the attention he was receiving.

"Having moments like this with horses, teaching them how to do things with us in an easy and safe manner, goes a long way towards building a relationship with any horse," said the Ole' Man. "Are you starting to understand how all of this comes together to help horses learn," asked the Ole' Man further.

"I think so," said the girl. "I can see Duke is really doing well. It makes sense to him, that's for sure."

"Let's find some shade and sit for a few minutes, and I'll try to review quickly what I consider to be some of the main points. In the next few days, it's going to be your responsibility to work with Duke to help make this training process really solid for him."

The girl and the Ole' Man found a place to sit in the shade over by the rock out cropping, and Duke found time to take a nap.

"What do you think so far, is Duke learning anything," inquired the Ole' Man.

"I think he is learning a lot and he seemed happy and relaxed, even becoming more confident in himself," said the girl.

"I am beginning to understand that the rider has to be very focused, and have a plan when working with a horse, so as not to confuse them. I realise that with using the rock as a focal point with repetition, and making sure you give the same consistent verbal commands, makes a big difference to Duke's learning process."

"Do you think the intermittent treats help teach or not," asked the Ole' Man.

"Oh yes, that seems really to help," said the girl, "I really thought he started to pay more attention, I think he tried harder."

"Congratulations," said the Ole' Man, "it sounds like maybe it's helping you as well."

"Let's not lose sight of a very important part of this teaching process, we want Duke willingly to go forward, always driving from his well engaged hocks and hind-end, as we asked him to do smooth transitions, while he freely flows forward around the circle."

"This helps condition the whole horse mentally, physically and emotionally, we really want to see the horse develop the ability to round up his top line. The result of that will show itself by Duke's head naturally becoming more vertical, as his conditioning and strength will improve."

"Never forget, just like your hands, the soft Side Reins and the bit are there to catch the energy flowing from the hind-end right through the horse's body, and not there to force or confine, but to direct the energy."

"This training process helps to produce a soft lower jaw and that's important, because if a horse is stiff in his lower jaw, he will be stiff throughout the rest of his body. Suppleness and softness in the bridle is what we are working towards."

"Not pulling and stiffness," added the Ole' Man.

"The ultimate goal is to have the horse physically well conditioned, by adopting a teaching programme, that mentally, physically and emotionally conditions the horse throughout the early stages of development. Primarily from the ground, this can only help enhance his natural athletic qualities, in preparation to carry a rider, while doing more demanding and complicated movements later on in his training."

"Light work in the arena and cross-country or trail riding, is also used to further condition the horse. The emphasis here will be to ride the horse forward while maintaining light contact only, allowing the horse to stretch and to lengthen his stride, to become fluid and move forward, and be straight. This entire conditioning programme is helping to further develop and strengthen the horse's legs, lungs and heart."

"This kind of exercise and riding complements the conditioning of the early ground work, either on the lunge line or utilising a fifty five foot round pen, or both."

"Let me try to wrap this up for you as a review," said the Ole' Man.

"We all want our horses to understand us, but the first thing we should strive to do, is to understand the horse as completely and fully as possible, and develop a deep and abiding respect for the complete subject, which is the training of the horse."

"All of the individual subjects we are teaching our horse should allow him to become better conditioned, as much as possible. This is to be done before we start to demand from him tasks that he is incapable of understanding, due to a lack of foundational training, or cannot physically perform the task when we ride him, because we have not taken the time to condition him physically first."

"Long before we place serious demands on our horses through riding them, we need to prepare the horse physically, mentally, emotionally and spiritually, through the complete foundational training programme."

"When we have completed that part of the journey with them, we would have established a solid relationship, and the horse would have acquired many skills at liberty, as we are doing presently with Duke. That is first and foremost, without that in place you have nothing to work from," stresses the Ole' Man.

"I hope that this is becoming clearer, that throughout this complete foundational training programme we take a building block approach, step by step."

"We are teaching the horse to do many things to our commands, recognise our individual body-language signals, as we work with him within the Circle of Knowledge and Truth. We are working with him to develop his conditioning through working with the Side Reins transitions, asking him to Whoa, giving him commands to do many things, so you have an opportunity to build a relationship with him."

"The horse, in the meantime, gets to be physically, mentally and emotionally better and better trained, in preparation for us to ride him at a more complicated level."

"Of Course," added the Ole' Man, "even during this early part of training we are going to ride the horse. It is just that we need to understand, that we are not going to place unreasonable demands on him, which the horse cannot understand, or he is not in the physical condition to do. If we pressure our horses too early we may cause masses of confusion with the horse, and develop a problem horse."

"We also get frustrated, we get upset, the horse gets upset and he just becomes a wreck."

"Within this programme, we give the horse the opportunity to learn many skills, and to be in better condition to develop himself physically, before we ride him too much. An example would be using the Side Reins, where we get to develop that nice soft jaw before riding him and being too aggressive in the face, which leads to many problems."

"Well," said the Ole' Man at last, "I think that's enough reviewing by me."

"Duke has really worked very well for us, he really tried hard to please you," said the Ole' Man.

"Yes," said the girl, "I think he did."

"I couldn't help notice that you have a small knapsack with you, did you happen to bring some sandwiches with you?"

"Yes, I did," said the girl. "Sometimes even when I am just on a trail ride, I take a snack with me and something to drink, and of course, a treat for Duke."

"You are very well organized, there are a couple of more little exercises I would like to show you and Duke today if I may, so why don't we sit here for a while, and give Duke this well deserved treat and you may have your snack."

During the time they sat together, the Ole' Man shared further horse related wisdom and knowledge with the girl.

Chapter 8

"Let's move on, what do you say?"

"You maybe thinking why bother to do the following exercise with Duke," mused the Ole' Man.

"Let me tell you, it helps to soften completely the horse's head, and lower the jaw and face. It stretches and conditions the neck muscles to both sides of the neck, which will allow you, when riding circles and lateral work, an ability to place your horse's head wherever you would like it to be, during many of your later and more complicated riding exercises."

"You can do this exercise anywhere, anytime, when your horse is cooling off, just sitting and relaxing maybe talking with friends. I do this, what I call, Mr. Supple Face exercise to develop lateral flexion," explained the Ole' Man.

"You'll find that you cannot do too much of it, you'll be the envy of your riding friends when they see how soft, giving and supple your horse has become throughout his head and neck."

"It will give you a great guiding or directional control, and a lightness in the lower jaw more than you have ever felt before."

"Please be patient with this little exercise, I know you and your horse will benefit greatly from it, and be the happier for it. Remember, that a horse that is soft in his lower jaw, will be soft throughout his whole body, tension will disappear, and stiffness in the shoulder and back will be a thing of the past."

"The whole ride will become more fluid, softer and forward."

"Let me try to explain some of the key elements of this exercise, so that it will work well for you," said the Ole' Man.

The Ole' Man started explaining in earnest and asked the girl to pay close attention.

"Always remember to maintain contact with what we are going to call the outside rein, or supporting rein. Let me define for you what the outside rein is, it is the rein that is not asking for the bend."

"So the other rein, the inside one, is the one that simply indicates to the horse to move his head in the direction you asked for, we can also call it the directing or bending rein."

"Our objective or intent here is to educate Duke to soften to, and become less dependent on the inside rein, while becoming educated to take direction that is being defined by the outside supporting rein, which will be supported by the use of riding more with your inside leg, at the girth or the cinch. This will help you understand the concept of riding more from your inside leg through to your outside rein, which as a matter of interest truly helps define for the horse the degree of curve throughout his entire body. This of course is most important, and is the only way to be able to ride great circles."

"Once you can ride your horse straight and complete perfect circles, you are well on your way to being able to position your horse anywhere you want. With this level of foundational control and the conditioning work you have already been doing, as soon as you and Duke want to try more complex movements, they should happen as a natural progression throughout this training program."

"Since it is a building block concept, success builds on success, as the horse is constantly being prepared for the next task or movement, it helps keep the stress levels down for the horse and you."

"This way you have a deep unshakeable foundation to grow constantly from."

"Should you find some days that things are not going as well, it does not matter, you can always do so many other things. You can revisit them, and then that becomes a proactive synergistic way to develop a positive growth pattern, one in which, the horse learns to become confident while being in a relaxed frame of mind, therefore receptive to learning some new tasks or skills."

"So often I find, that people are totally confusing their horses by asking them to try to do something, which is way beyond their present skill level, without the benefit of preparing and making them proficient at the lower preceding skill level."

"It's like asking a baby to run a mile in five minutes and yet, today the baby has just started to crawl."

"How does that relate to riding circles," asked the girl.

"Good question," said the Ole' Man.

"Let me try to give you a very simple example. Riding a good well defined circle at any gait is a requirement, let's call it foundational, to be able to ride other movements."

"Let's agree that most people know what it feels like to ride in a car, let's assume we are going to drive it slowly on a large circle. We start off, but halfway around, Bang! We get a completely and totally flat tire. Try as we may to pull on the steering wheel, the flat tire is pulling us all over the place, the front-end is out of balance, it wanders all over the place, as we fight with it to readjust, to keep the car on the circle, we lose control, come off the circle and yet still wander around. Get the idea," asked the Ole' Man.

"I'm not sure," said the girl.

"The horse front feet are a bit like our car's front tires. They need to be light and free to move as required, so we do not want or need them to become heavy and sticking in the ground. We can cause this by pulling or having too much contact with our inside rein, too much bend then will cause too much weight over that shoulder and down to that foot, making it like a flat tire."

"Duke will do other things to adjust to it, like adjusting his rib cage, and even the shoulders or hind legs will start to compensate, so he can be rebalanced, but in doing so he's going to wiggle around and that will make riding a nice circle very difficult for you, and quite frustrating for Duke."

"I do want you to realise that it is important to understand that Duke's training progresses, as you'll be learning how to control and influence his rib cage and hind-end, by using what we call driving aids of our seat and legs."

"At this time, just use this exercise to help develop and educate Duke to a softness and acceptance of the contact and direction through your hands to the bit in Duke's mouth. He is comfortable with that at this level, which is at first just standing still at the centre of our clock-face circle. We'll do this before we go on to walk the circle, and then later on progress from that to canter, it makes a great deal of sense to have control over Duke's face first."

"Therefore, I think it makes a lot of sense to me and Duke that we should have an agreement or understanding, a willing acceptance that he will place his head slightly in the direction that you ask him to go."

"In doing so, we will not end up having a tug-of-war, a pulling match, or a fight going on. It's only fair to Duke to educate him quietly while standing still, before we even think of trying to canter him."

"Unfortunately most people do not do so, then the horse who is trying to evade pain in his face, starts to do all sorts of things, like throwing his head around, dropping his shoulder into the circle, in fact, anything but maintaining a nice circle."

"Of course, all those things are happening, because we did not take the time, or had the patience to educate the horse to be soft and accepting directions through the reins, that of course he would understand and be willing to follow that guidance. Are you and Duke ready to get started on this next quite easy to do exercise? I call it Mr. Supple Face, and use it as a lateral flexion exercise."

"Yes," said the girl looking very interested, as she mounted Duke.

"Just walk over here to the centre of the circle and ask Duke to Whoa, I'll walk over with you," instructed the Ole' Man.

Duke was happy to stand still, the Ole' Man stroked Duke's neck and told him he was a good boy, he attached his piece of rope to the halter while explaining to the girl, that he was going to be there with her, to lend a helping hand if necessary.

"OK, as you sit here I want you to imagine that you and Duke are standing in the middle of a large clock-face, and just were Duke's head is facing, he is looking straight at 12 o'clock, am I making that clear?"

"Big clock-face," said the girl, "What for?"

"It's easy," said the Ole' Man, "you'll see, remember Duke's nose is pointing at the 12 o'clock direction. To start with, we are going to supple him to his right, by imagining where 1, 2 and finally 3 o'clock are, which will be when Duke nose comes all the way around to just about the tip of your boot, as your leg hangs naturally under you, that should give you a rough idea for now."

"Let's review it before we go on with the exercise. Duke has had time really to learn and develop feel for the contact of light pressure, that I have set up for him with Side Reins. Duke has been given time to learn how to adjust his head during transitions and when coming to a stop. We can both see he is confident and relaxed at this level of training, if he was not, we would, of course, carry on with Side Reins until he would show that he was ready to move along in his training."

"Many signs would help indicate that Duke was comfortable with what we are asking him to do, he would be relaxed and calm in his work sessions, willing to work with us, eyes blinking, mouth chewing and saliva dripping out of his mouth."

"Do you think Duke is ready to learn something new, which will also help keep him interested in what we are doing," asked the Ole' Man.

"Yes," said the girl. "I think I recognise that Duke is ready to move on in his training, and in what we are asking him to do."

"What else do you think," inquired the Ole' Man.

"I am not sure," said the girl, "usually when I pick up one rein all Duke does is turnaround my leg in small tight circles."

"Good answer," said the Ole' Man, "but we are going to teach Duke something different now, this is so exciting," said the Ole' Man.

"Let's get started, we are going to do this very slowly, there's no rush, we want Duke not to become confused, so he will learn quickly. While we present your signals or instructions so clearly and he understands, and even at first just trying, you'll reward him immediately, by just softening the pressure that you applied when you asked him to follow with his nose, in this case it will be your right rein – right-handed."

"But what am I going to be doing, how am I going to get his nose to 1 o'clock," enquired the girl.

"Relax, you can do it," said the Ole' Man, "do not worry, I am going to talk you through the whole thing, as I said – it easy."

"Now, I want you to pick up both of your reins slowly, smoothly, and have your hands at waist height out in front of you about halfway towards the base of your horse's neck, just keep your hands down, the reins quietly, there, that's great."

"I would like you to try to feel both sides of Duke's mouth through your contact with his snaffle-bit. Try not to have more contact on one side or the other, so you give him the clear message just to keep his head straight at this time. I am just going to help steady Duke's head by holding the halter, just while you get the feel of it."

"Can you feel both sides of his mouth in your fingers?"

The girl didn't seem to be sure, frowned at the Ole' Man and said, "I am not sure if I can feel that, or if I ever have."

"Relax," said the Ole' Man. "Lower both of your hands, just to give them a little slack, there, that's good."

"I want you to trust me, close your eyes for a moment, then just sit deep in your seat and let all the tension in your body go away and breathe deeply for a few minutes. I'll be here at Duke's head, so do not worry he will not go anywhere, but he will feel what you are doing, Duke will pick up on that. When you become relaxed and supporting of what we are going to ask him to do, he will understand that, and he needs that from you, relax, you are doing very well."

The girl sighed as a response to the Ole' Man encouragement.

"Keep your eyes closed, this time I want you to just squeeze your reins in your hands like you would squeeze water out of a sponge. Good, do it two or three times, it is like whispering Hello to Duke to let him know something is about to change."

"Do it one more time, and then take all the slack out of reins by moving your hands just a little, you should be able to feel both sides of Duke's mouth." The girl slowly moved her hands and lightly came into contact with Duke's lips, he pushed just a little into her hands testing, and her hands stayed steady, Duke softened and the girl smiled.

"Open your eyes," said the Ole' Man elated. "Well done both of you, I watched Duke's lips and eyes, he was pretty comfortable with that, now, that is an experience you can build on at home. Do it a lot to develop that level of feel, that level of contact between you."

"Could you feel both sides of his mouth," asked the Ole' Man.

"Oh yes," said the girl, "it felt so soft, I never felt that before on any horse." The girl let her reins rest on Duke's neck, then with the reins in her right hand, she reached forward to stroke his neck with her left hand, "Good Boy Duke, you are so smart, Good Boy."

Duke's feet had not moved at all indicating, that the girl really had his attention, he was there with her enjoying the joint new experience, awaiting the next request, enjoying the reward of the loose rein and the gentle strokes, to him it felt good and it was all starting to make sense.

"Well, I think we are really ready to move onto the next stage, are you ready."

"I can hardly wait," said the girl. "I want to teach Duke how to move his nose to that 1 o'clock position, what do I have to do? Please tell me, I know Duke and I are ready and we can do it."

"This is great," said the Ole' Man. "It's going so well, I am so proud of both of you, let's go on."

"I'll talk you through it. Remember to start with me, we are going to be working to your right towards 1 o'clock, ready?"

"Yes," said the girl, "let's do it."

"I'll give you a quick outline then we will go through it." The Ole' Man paused just for a moment and carried on explaining.

"Firstly, it's very important to understand that your left rein is going to be a supporting rein. This means you need to maintain constant contact, and to follow the left side of Duke's face and bit. Since that side of his neck stretches, as his nose moves to the right, as you are asking it by bringing your right hand out a little wide, and then back towards your right hip."

"At this level of training, you have as much pressure as is required, to have Duke move his head. It could be two ounces, four pounds, or forty pounds, always try to keep it as light and soft as possible, but If needed, you must increase the pressure until Duke understands to move, and move he must. Even if it's only a small try, you must reward him immediately by softening, or releasing your right rein contact, from the pressure you were applying to neutral, which will become supporting."

"When I use the term releasing, it does not mean throwing the rein completely away, that would be too confusing for Duke, but soften so he can distinguish between an even firm constant pull saying Duke move your head to here, and when he is at 1 o'clock, you immediately soften and yet be in a supporting passive state. This is his instant reward, and that must happen, so Duke will understand and learn, it will make sense to him."

"I think that is all, for the main part of this exercise, it is really easy to do, as long as you understand the 'why' of it, and remember to be consistent."

"All right, do you have any other questions, have I made myself clear," asked the Ole' Man finally.

"Very clear," said the girl. "I think I've really got it, I see how some of these pieces all come together, and it is important not to miss out some of it during the training process."

"From the beginning," said the Ole' Man getting really quite excited. "Pickup both reins softly, squeezed and vibrate them in your hands, it will cause your reins to come alive, as they say to Duke Hello, wake up, pay attention, something different is about to happen, I am going to give you a new message."

"All right," said the girl, smiling, now much more relaxed and confident.

"Feel both sides of his mouth."

"Got it," said the girl.

"What's next," asked the Ole' Man.

"I am going to keep constant contact and follow with my left rein, and I am going to pick up the constant firm pull with my right hand going a little wide and back toward my right hip until I get Duke, as closed as I can, to the 1 o'clock position. It feels pretty light," said the girl as Duke's nose started to move.

"Good," said the Ole' Man. "Keep it up, follow with that left supporting outside rein, that's good, you look to 1 o'clock as well, that will help Duke, keep moving your head and your hands, keep supporting and remain active with constant contact on your right rein." Duke was coming around really well he was trying hard, he was there and all the previous work and relationship-building was starting to pay off.

"You going to make it," said the Ole' Man, "keep his head moving, just keep asking, now when you get to what you think is 1 o'clock, then soften your active inside right rein, and just become passive with it, remain there supporting and soften, and then from that moment – that will be Duke's reward, as you just become passive and supportive with that right rein, because he is now at the place that you want him to be."

The Girl stopped at 1 o'clock.

Duke thought it was a good idea to try simply to take his head back to where it came from. The Ole' Man was ahead of this game and almost before Duke started this trick, he said to the girl "Be ready to hold your right rein there, like saying to Duke NO! Duke I want you to keep your head here."

Duke tried this a couple of times, and the girl would just give and take with that right inside rein, while continuing to maintain a supportive passive contact with her outside left rein.

"Well done, that went very well," said the Ole' Man stroking Duke's neck. "Seeing that Duke seemed so happy, go ahead and move his nose to 2 o'clock now, are you ready for that?"

"Yes," said the girl, "let's go on to 2 o'clock."

"Talk yourself through it, and just tell me what's happening," said the Ole' Man. "I'll be here to help, first just vibrate the reins and let Duke know that something is about happen, that you are going to give him a new command."

"Right," said the girl, "here it goes, I am squeezing my rein to say Hello Duke. Should I look towards 2 o'clock?"

"Yes. Good point," said the Ole' Man, "always look towards where you are going."

"Duke is a little stiffer here, now almost braced to the right rein, what do I do," asked the girl.

"That's fine," said the Ole' Man, "become more active with your right rein, apply more even-constant pressure until Duke tries, or starts to move, of course, continue to follow to give him room to move with that all-important supporting left rein."

Duke moved his head back and forth between 1 o'clock and 2 o'clock. It was a constant game of give and take, a pressure and less pressure, to soften and be passive. To apply more pressure, to keep moving Duke towards 2 o'clock, it only took a few minutes of this, and Duke was there at 2 o'clock.

The girl softened immediately, the Ole' Man immediately stroked Duke's neck, "Good Boy Duke, Good Boy, you are so smart."

Duke stayed at 2 o'clock, his eyes almost closed, they were so soft.

"I want you now to move him back to 12 o'clock, while you do your best to keep Duke balanced between both reins and place his head straight in front of his shoulders, go ahead."

Duke was a little stiff, but it went quite well, when at 12 o'clock the Ole' Man had the girl just held there for a few moments on contact, then slowly supporting Duke's head in the natural position he had placed it. The girl then softened the contact and Duke started to reach out with his head and neck.

"Keep feeding the reins to him until he stops reaching," said the Ole' Man. "He is now actually reaching for the contact of the bit, so we do not want to throw it away just yet, that would be too much, too confusing for Duke."

Duke's head was half way to the ground when he stopped.

"There," said the Ole' Man, "just hold passive there for a moment, then give him a full loose rein by placing your hands on his withers and place the reins in one hand reach forward, stroke his neck and withers and praise him a lot."

Duke gave a big exhale, snorted and licked his lips, and then he fully stretched out his head and neck.

"There," said the Ole' Man, "Did you hear that, that's Duke telling us that he understands now, and he is comfortable with what we are teaching him."

"Yes, Good Boy Duke, I am so proud of you," said the girl quite excited.

"I am happy and proud of you," said the Ole' Man. "It went very well, preparation is so important, giving Duke the required time to learn the concept of softening to light pressure of the Side Reins, helped lay the foundation for this exercise."

"I must say, your timing and feel through the reins was excellent, you had the required level of constant firmness and in directing him to a certain position, and your timing was just right on, when needed, as you softened with your right rein, just being there supporting and being passive, and that required moment makes so much sense to Duke. It's his reward, our way of saying to Duke well done, you are getting this right."

"If Duke could talk, he would be saying OK, I got it, you take up contact, direct me to a place or a position, when I comply you reward my effort by becoming soft and supporting, trusting me to stay where you asked my nose to be. It becomes an agreement between us, and we can continue to build our relationship on that level of respect for each other, but until we have that, we really have little or nothing to build on."

"Are you starting to feel the difference, not only in Duke's mouth, but in his change of attitude," inquired the Ole' Man.

The girl was smiling as she answered "Oh yes, I can feel the difference, and I'm feeling a lot different about Duke. I realise now, that most of the time, he really was trying for me, and sometimes I was just asking too much of him. I confused him with my conflicting signals, or at times, my constant pulling with no release."

"That's wonderful, that you have realised so much already, I think you have reached a breakthrough in understanding how to present things to Duke, and help make it as easy as possible for him to succeed. You may ask now, by never asking him to do something he does not, at least in part, understand, so what we do is keep taking small steps and presenting things to Duke, and in that way we keep building on something that he gets to understand."

"Let's just spend a few more minutes asking Duke to move his head again to the 1 and 2 o'clock positions. If it goes well, let's move on to that full bend to the 3 o'clock. This will really stretch the left side to the maximum, while causing the right inside neck muscles to shorten, or compress somewhat. That's what also makes this into a good exercise, the stretching and compressing of the neck muscles in both directions, to supple the horse."

"I want you to just sit there for a few moments breathing deeply, close your eyes, and relax," instructed the Ole' Man.

"Now, visualise you and Duke going through this complete exercise to the right. Feel it at a high level of excellence, as Duke willingly complies with your soft intent for him to move his nose to the required position. In fact, I just want you to sit here for a moment and actually think that he, Duke, already put his nose at the 1 o'clock, 2 o'clock and then went to the 3 o'clock position. Imagine that he complied with all that you asked of him, and that he has already done it to a level of excellence that you would expect. Believe that you are now already happy and smiling with the results. This way, even before we go ahead and perform it, you have the concept in your mind that you've actually seen him do it. You've felt him do it. It has already happened, and you are happy and confident."

"Take a deep breath and go through this exercise, see it and feel it, as you've prepared and planned it in your mind, including every response you are to have. When you are ready, open your eyes, and with full confidence in a relaxed manner, complete this exercise."

The girl went through this mind exercise, while Duke stood quietly on a loose rein with the Ole' Man standing off just to one side of Duke's shoulder. After a few minutes the girl opened her eyes and took another deep breath, quietly picked up her reins vibrated them – "Hello Duke."

Smoothly, the girl took Duke through the motions. It went really well until Duke was asked to move past the 2 o'clock position, he got a little stuck there, which would be expected at this level of training. The Ole' Man encouraged her to keep asking Duke, by applying more firmness and pressure to her right rein, and as Duke moved in response, to soften immediately. In this way, the girl was able, in stages, to progress with Duke from 2 o'clock, until Duke was just about touching his nose on the toe of the girl's right boot.

The girl was thrilled with Duke. "Good Boy, Duke. What a smart boy you are."

"Put your right rein in your left hand and stroke Duke's forehead with your right hand," instructed the Ole' Man, as Duke just relaxed there in the 3 o'clock position.

"Alright," said the girl and stroked Duke's forehead. He stayed at the 3 o'clock position. "Good Boy." She continued to stroke him and Duke was so relaxed, he closed his eyes and stayed right there.

"That's wonderful," said the Ole' Man. "Now you are, again by stages, going to return Duke to the 12 o'clock position. Now let us pick up equal contact with both reins, vibrate both your reins to say Hello to Duke, to let him know something else is about to happen. Apply slightly more pressure to the left rein to direct Duke's nose all the way back to the 12 o'clock position."

"Remember to be supporting with the now right rein, then stop Duke at 2 o'clock using your right rein, hold there until he softens, then you softened and apply a little more pressure with your left rein, continue to control, with the soft supporting right rein, the following more active left rein."

"Go all the way through to 2 o'clock, and stop Duke right there. Feel both sides of his mouth balanced and supporting, good. Now repeat as before, move your hands forward and now slowly towards his withers, slowly supporting and allowed Duke to search for the contact of the bit as he follows your hands forward down, and keep feeding him both reins and the feel of your hands right up to him, finding a comfortable place to stop, at this time – it's his choice."

"When he stops searching for the contact of the bit, I want you just to hold there, at that level of feel, just for a moment, for both of you to feel the experience," said the Ole' Man.

"He has stopped searching," said the girl, "and I can feel both sides of his mouth."

"Great," said the Ole' Man. "I can see that it has happened. Now slowly feed him the rest of your reins and place your hands on his withers, and then hold the reins in one hand and continue to praise him, reach forward and stroke his neck."

The girl was smiling broadly. Duke snorted and shook his head from side to side and gave a big exhale.

"This is wonderful," said the Ole' Man, "let Duke just stand and rest here to process what he has just learned, keep stroking and praising him to reward him, so it reinforces both the good physical and emotional experience that he's just have been a part of."

"Before I forget," said the Ole' Man, "we worked Duke's head to the right. Do not forget to work both sides, and of course, if you should find some little tough spots, just take your time and work more on these areas. Your main intent, or goal, is to have Duke equally supple in both directions," ended the Ole' Man.

After a few more minutes of the Ole' Man and the girl continuing to praise and reward Duke with strokes to his neck and withers, the Ole' Man said "Well, that really went so well. Duke was really kind and trying. You are doing really well and I am so proud of both of you."

"How would you like to dismount for a few minutes, so I can show you another little exercise I call it Vertical Flexion in Halter, and it takes just a few minutes per day, you can easily do it while you groom Duke, or as we are doing just standing around, taking a little break."

"I am going to teach Duke to lower his head to the lightest pressure possible just using a halter and the lead shank; it has many benefits, one being that it makes it a lot easier to bridle Duke if he will lower his head for you. This exercise will also help build the foundation for learning to yield to pressure when you apply it. That will help with teaching Duke to tie, and learn the concept of vertical flexion."

"You can add in the occasional treat for Duke if you want to, this will help to increase his learning curve."

"This is easy to do, and I am confident Duke can do this, it's so important for me to be in the right frame of mind before I start. That I have a reasonable expectation that Duke will really try for me."

"However, I understand and respect that Duke is not going to get this, or anything else that I try to teach him, right on the first time, so when Duke has some resistance I accept that. At that moment, Duke has just not quite fully understood what I wanted from him. I do not think he is being a bad horse, or that he is just trying to spoil my day," explained the Ole' Man.

"My attitude is that Duke is searching, he is trying to understand what I want, and so I must always give him the benefit of the doubt, recognising the slightest degree of try, to reward him for it immediately. The reward for horses often will come in the form of less pressure being applied. We will often use the expression: soften the contact, much more on this later."

"All of these little items of training or teaching should always be there, so you have something to build on, or to progress from, step-by-step."

"That's one of the secrets of teaching horses anything."

"Well, yet again maybe I've talked too much, Duke looks calm and relaxed; he does have his snaffle bridle on, with a halter over it. I'll attach your lead shank to the centre ring at his jaw, I'll stand just off to one side and in front of Duke left shoulder," continued the Ole' Man.

"My left hand is going to hold about eight inches below his jaw. The remainder of the lead shank I'll lay over the crook of the elbow of my left arm, like this. Now my right hand, I am going to place it up here, right behind Duke's ears, just like this, and I am going to stroke him here for a few minutes."

"Since I know Duke likes that, and it will help him relaxed and get him to the right mental state of mind to respond to me."

"I hope I am making myself clear, that taking the time to prepare the horse properly is very important, so we set him up for success, and all he has to do is at least try. Then we must quickly praise and reward him ASAP."

"Following this path to learning, reduces stress and confusion for the horse; a confused horse cannot learn. When stressed too much, Duke will have no other choice but to revert to self-preservation mode, that's always high on his list, then he'll no longer be with us, the connection that we did have, will now be broken."

"Let's give Duke something to do, I think he is ready, what about you," the Ole' Man said to the girl.

"Yes," said the girl, "Duke looks really ready he is relaxed and his eyes are half closed, I think you'll have to wake him up."

"That's what I want," said the Ole' Man, "I'll talk my way through this, and you can observe how Duke responds."

"I am just going to shake the lead shank lightly to wake Duke up, and stroke him on the neck, Good Boy Duke, wake up, and then I am going to place my right hand back up here behind the ears there, now Duke and I are ready for the next part."

"With my left hand, as you can see, I am starting to apply light pressure straight down; Duke has gone a little stiff offering resistance, because he does not understand yet that I want him to lower his head. If I applied more pressure or pull hard, I could actually cause what I do not want to teach Duke to do, and that would be for Duke to pull back. Therefore, as you can see I am just holding here at this level of contact or pressure on the halter, waiting, giving Duke an opportunity to soften not to even lower his head, but just to soften even the slightest for me."

"As you can see Duke is searching by moving his head from side to side, and I'm doing my best to follow wherever he moves his head to, while I try to maintain the same feel and level of pressure, but not pulling on him. I need to be constant, firm and steady in the application of my instructions to him."

"I'm going to give Duke a few minutes break and then I am going to start again, Good Boy Duke, relax."

"Could you see how Duke didn't understand what I was asking of him, and how he was resisting," asked the Ole' Man.

"Yes, I think so," said the girl, "I could see in his eye that he was not sure what to do, and so he seemed just to move around."

"Yes, good," said the Ole' Man, "that's correct, lets try again, Good Boy Duke, are you ready, I am now applying the same pressure again and I am going to stroke behind his ears at the same time. This time with my left hand I'm going to wait a few minutes, and then I am going to soften; now there, now I am going to apply the same pressure again and wait."

"There, did you see that Duke softened a little, so I softened, Good Boy Duke," praised the Ole' Man happy to see even the slight response from Duke.

"Again, the same pressure straight down, Duke softens, I soften but I do not completely let go, I maintain my feel with light passive contact."

"Watch, on again with the pull down and Duke lowers his head, Good Boy Duke, and I am rubbing behind his ears as a further reward to my softening, you see that Duke is blinking and chewing, he is catching on."

"My goal is to get as low as I can, by applying the pressure on. Then softened the pressure and have what I call a passive contact as a reward, then stroke his neck like this and praise him Good Boy Duke, how smart you are."

"OK, as you can see Duke's head is lower and I continued to support him by rubbing behind his ears."

"Now again, I am going to apply the same level of pressure while asking him to soften to that, I am giving and taking with my left hand showing Duke the way to the ground."

"Just one more time, light pressure to say lower, Duke moves a couple of inches, I soften my pressure to a passive contact, which is supporting and rewarding."

"Then I'll hold here just for a moment, while stroking Duke's neck Good Boy Duke, Good Boy."

"Watch now, as I'm going to take my left hand away from his jaw area, and move it to the end of the lead shank, and just let Duke feel the weight difference, as I continue to stroke his neck with my right hand and praise him, Good Boy Duke, what a smart boy."

The Ole' Man then, while standing along side Duke's shoulders, turned into the position to lead Duke. Then said "Duke, Walk-on," the Ole' Man walked away quite quickly and Duke followed, he made about a thirty foot circle and came back to the same spot in the centre.

"Duke Whoa," as the Ole' Man stopped so did Duke.

"There," said the Ole' Man, turning once again to face Duke's shoulder and stroking it, "Good Boy Duke, well done, you really did try lots Duke."

"Doing a couple of circles and coming back to the same place, and then repeating the exercise is a good thing to do."

"It gives Duke a break but helps keep him interested, and then you can make a fresh start with the exercise again, when you are ready and you take the time to set Duke up for it."

"Well, I think that's about all I can show you, it takes longer to explain it than it does to practice it, and that's the good news, I am sure you'll do fine with it. I have just got Duke started for you."

"If you are patient and consistent with him, I am sure the next time I'll see you and Duke you should be able to put his nose on the ground. I know you can do that, what do you think and can you see some real benefit in this exercise for you and Duke," asked the Ole' Man.

The girl smiled at the Ole' Man. "Oh yes, sometimes Duke would lift his head high when I would try to bridle him, so this will help. Sometimes while leading, he has pulled back on me and braced, so it just became a pulling contest, I always lost. Duke would step back and pull me forward, so teaching him in anyway to soften to pressure, I guess will help. Will it help with riding as well," inquired the girl.

"Everything we do builds towards another level or degree of difficulty in the training process and ultimately towards improving the riding, so to answer your question, yes."

"You see there is so much we can teach our horses to do from the ground, in conjunction with riding them," reminded the Ole' Man.

"Of course, I agree," said the girl, and then turning to Duke. "Duke what a smart boy you are, he really is learning quickly when you are teaching him like you are, it's so different and yet I can see the results in Duke, and he seemed to be so happy with you. I think he even enjoys doing things with you."

"Well, that's the way it should be," said the Ole' Man. "Let me put it this way, with regards to providing a positive learning environment, you and the driving instructor are sitting in a car in the middle of a large parking lot. The Instructor starts to give you all kinds of information about how to take the car through the gears, at certain speeds. Now you are getting directions to go this way and that way. You start to feel the anger and the frustration from the instructor, who is by now shouting at you, you opened the door and jump out, and run a few yards away from the car, confuse and afraid. The instructor walks over to you and starts to say to you 'tell me, why don't you follow my instructions and drive the car out of this parking lot."

And you answer in frustration, "because you never gave me the key to start the car."

The girl laughed.

"Sometimes," said the Ole' Man, "we forget to give the horse the key."

"By that I mean, we seem to often miss small but very important little pieces of information. Then the horse becomes, what I call, developmentally stuck, because areas in a logical training sequence have been neglected, or worse, missed altogether."

"Consequently this makes it very hard, if not impossible for many horses to advance to certain levels, because we have not provided the horse with all the steps or parts he needs. Like you not getting the car key, but here is a really funny thing, horses never have any problems moving around, until we attempt to ride them."

"Let me ask you this, have you ever had the opportunity to see horses running free in a field," asked the Ole' Man.

"Yes, I have a couple of times, why," said the girl.

"For the reason that it would seem to me that horses are more than capable of doing anything that most riders would like them to do, without them – the riders I mean."

"Often we are too quick to assume the horse is the problem, and yet, twenty minutes before we arrived at the barn to ride and therefore control his movements, he was actually doing just fine, playing with his friends."

"The horse was cantering fairly nice circles on the correct lead, at times even doing counter canter and serpentines."

"Then an effortless transition to a floating fluid forward extended trot, neck arched, head nearing the vertical, the horse being driven by a deep driving hind-end, producing a horse in a nice frame with a well rounded top line. Front feet light and free at last, to be placed and moved again at the command of the horse's supple shoulders.

"The horse does what horses were built to do – to run, turn circles to stop quickly and to do a roll back, now the horse runs to the corner of the fence line and completes, in part, a canter pirouette and comes out of it on the correct lead, drives off his hind legs, to continue to go forward with uninhibited free elastic fluid movement."

"Long long ago, our forefathers watched these magnificent majestic creatures do such movements at liberty, and dreamt of being a part of it."

"I still do, what about you," asked the Ole' Man.

"Maybe becoming like a Centaur, half man – half horse, or becoming fully integrated with the horse. Being able to be a part of and yet control what I would like the horse to do for me, through my seat, legs and body and with much less influence of my hands," added the Ole' Man.

"It does not matter who caused it, or where and when we strayed off the path to true knowledge about communicating with our horses. The good news is, today right now, we have an opportunity to change, to grow, and we all have a choice, to do things differently."

"First you have to recognise that you want to change, because if you want your horse to change on the outside, *you* must first change from within, and realise you have free will and the power to do all that it required to change your future with your horse."

"This does sound a bit complicated," said the girl, "yes, I want things to change for Duke and me, but how do I achieve that."

"That's a very interesting question, and one we will have to address some other time.

The Ole' Man wanted to share with them one more little exercise to help produce confidence in the bridle. For Duke, this was an exercise that would still help in being able to position his head and neck anywhere, as required by the girl. At the same time, still helping to develop a level of feel in the bridle for both of them, something they could both respect and understand.

"OK young lady, it's time for you to get back on Duke," said the Ole' Man.

"I would like to take just a few more minutes and share one more little skill with you. I know now is the time to do this with you both. Would that be acceptable to you? A few more minutes to finish off, then I believe it's time for you to start heading for home," said the Ole' Man.

"Yes, that would be fine," said the girl, "and you are right; I should head for home soon."

"Now, I'm going to show you how to have Duke raise and lower his head and neck, to add to what we have just finished."

"In the next couple of days at home, continue with both of these exercises it will make a huge difference, as you and Duke progress to other movements. It will really help to establish a way to ride and direct nice circles, and will, in time and with patience, all come together. You mustn't forget that teaching the horse is a journey."

Duke was enjoying doing nothing for a while, snoozing in the warmth of the day, resting and relaxing. The Ole' Man looked at Duke, stroked his neck gently and said, "OK big boy, you're doing so well and you are so smart. This will only take a few minutes of your valuable time. I know you're ready and you can do this, so wake up."

Duke's eyes were all but closed, his head and neck with his nose poked out were level to his top line, and his back left-hind was cocked resting.

"Well," said the Ole' Man, "Duke is certainly happy and relaxed, what about you young lady?"

"Yes, I am very happy with Duke," said the girl.

"And so you should be," said the Ole' Man, "and proud too, no doubt."

"Yes," said the girl, "he's changed so much already. Shall I go-ahead and pick up my reins and squeeze and see if I can wake Duke up?"

"Yes," said the Ole' Man, "Just like you did before quietly and evenly. Pick up the reins, vibrate them, and make them come alive in your hands."

Duke blinked, placed weight on his hind leg and rebalanced himself, then picked up his head and neck a little.

"Good. I think Duke is rejoining us. Hello Duke, Welcome back," said the Ole' Man.

Standing by Duke's left shoulder, the Ole' Man looked up at the girl and started to speak, giving her a general outline.

"Have I been able to make that pretty clear to you, and are you comfortable with the information, so we can begin?"

"Yes," said the girl, "but could you just talk me through it, at least for the first time?"

"No problem," said the Ole' Man. "Let's move on and get started."

"I am ready," said the girl.

"Fine," said the Ole' Man, "Just creep about half way down your reins and have your hands at a comfortable height for you, about half way between your waist and Duke's neck. At this level, for today, I'm going to make this as simple and direct as I can. Start to bring your hands slowly and quietly back towards your body until you can feel again both sides of Duke's face. Can you feel that?"

"Yes I can."

"Good. Hold it there," said the Ole' Man.

"Make sure you're sitting nice and deep in the saddle, giving yourself a secure strong place to be. I want you now to continue slowly and smoothly, with equal constant and active contact, to keep lifting your hands up and back to your shoulders."

The girl continued to shift her hands. Duke started to fuss a little and move his head a little bit from side to side, as his head reluctantly came up.

"Good," said the Ole' Man. "Keep lifting, be determined, keep equal contact on both sides of his face, keep moving your hands to maintain that balance of feel of both sides. Just move with the feel of it. Your job is to support Duke in his effort to seek the contact. How does that feel?"

"Not bad. I do not have that much pressure in my hands, but it is a bit hard to keep following," said the girl.

"You're doing fine," said the Ole' Man. "Let's bring his head and neck a little higher. I'll tell you when to stop and then hold him there."

"OK," said the girl.

Duke's neck was now higher than it would be when he was standing naturally.

"Good," said the Ole' Man. "Stop there, hold both sides of the bit equally and follow his head, if he moves. Good. Do not let him put his head back down, until we are ready. Let's try to get him to settle and accept this position and the contact."

Duke moved his head and neck around for a few minutes and twisted his face from side to side, but the girl was disciplined and determined to do her best. In no time Duke was starting to get the idea, paused and then stopped moving.

"That's it exactly," cried the Ole' Man. "That's the moment we have been waiting for, now soften, just be there, supporting, let Duke feel the contact."

"Has Duke become light in your hands? He's not pulling is he? He looks soft in your hands. Would you agree," asked the Ole' Man.

"Oh yes," said the girl smiling again. "He is really quite light right now."

"Good," said the Ole' Man, "then let's move on quickly to take advantage of this moment. Squeeze your reins and start to smoothly lower your hands. Duke will start to feel that, and he will follow your hands, as he seeks the supporting contact of your hands. Good, just keep feeding him the reins as you lower your hands."

"When Duke's head and neck get to the position that you would normally ride in, just stop."

"There, that's it, let Duke feel and settle into your hands. That looks good, right about there, so hold your hands just there. Do not let Duke pull you out of your position, that's why you need a firm secure seat, so you are in a position of strength, from which you can independently use your hands."

Duke fussed a little, but nothing too bad. The girl maintained her seat without too much difficulty.

"Well done, well done," said the Ole' Man, "Squeeze – vibrate your reins again to let Duke know something is going to happen, and then I want you to move your hands forward and begin lowering them, so Duke will want to follow and keep contact with the bit, which you are going to support gradually by moving your hands forward and down."

The girl moved her hands, Duke followed, lower and lower.

"Keep feeding him more reins until I tell you to stop, ready?"

The girl was concentrating hard. "Ready," she said.

"Stop," said the Ole' Man. "Hold your hands still and quiet."

Duke stopped going down, he just chewed on the bit and licked his lips.

"Just hold there for a moment," said the Ole' Man. "Let Duke feel that. Good. Squeeze your reins. There, now gradually and slowly start to raise your hands. Good. How does Duke feel in your hands?"

"Very light," replied the girl.

"That's what we want, Good Boy Duke," said the Ole' Man.

"Continue to bring your hands back to that place that they were. That's normal head and neck carriage position for Duke when you ride him. Go ahead and then stop, and hold him there."

Duke again followed the light, active and equal rein pressure that was being offered, and willingly stopped, maintaining his head position, when the rein ceased and became a supportive passive rein. He was learning the difference, and could even reach for the contact and become very light.

"Great," said the Ole' Man. "Maintain that level of contact just light, hold him there. Support Duke in his choice to be steady in this position, that's his reward, when you become passive and support him with your reins."

"He is doing what you requested, so why not just leave him alone. Then, he gets to understand if there's no active pressure, I'll just stay here in this position until asked to do something different."

"I hope this helps and it's starting to make sense to you," said the Ole' Man.

"Oh yes," replied the girl. "For most of the time, Duke is quite light. He pulled and pushed into my hands a couple of times, but I could just feel that when I stayed firm and steady, he would soften, and then I could just soften and support him at that point. There would be then very little weight or pressure in my hands, it's a wonderful feeling. Before this exercise it seemed like we were pulling against each other all the time, in fact, my shoulders used to hurt after most of my rides. I often felt like I was holding up his front-end and it was not much fun."

"Well," said the Ole' Man, "it does take two to pull."

"The trick is to learn that you may have to be firm with a steady pull. Duke may pull on you, but you have to hold firm and wait till he gives or softens his pull. Then, you must always immediately soften to him, as soon as possible, then and only then will he learn not to pull."

"Pulling against each other all the time only teaches Duke how to pull, or lean into your hands all the time. You, in fact, start to hold him up, you become the third leg of his front-end. Does that make sense to you, because I know it does to Duke?"

"Yes, it's starting to make a lot of sense," said the girl.

"That's great. I believe these exercises will help both of you build and strengthen your confidence in each other. I think you have a fair amount of work to do during the next couple of days. It's getting late. You should be going home, what do you say?"

"Yes, I have a lot to think about and do with Duke, you're right, I need to start for home," said the girl.

"I would like you to keep doing the good work you have been doing. Continue with working the Side Reins, exercising Duke, taking some nice relaxing trail rides on light contact, and some occasional treats. Also, I want you to add-in these exercises, as much as you can, would you do that for me and Duke?"

"Yes, I'll do as much as I can," said the girl.

The Ole' Man stroked Duke's neck. "Good Boy, Duke. I am so proud of you, you tried so hard to please, thank you."

"Would you still be available for further help, if Duke and I should run into challenges," inquired the girl.

"I know you and Duke will be doing just fine, but do not worry, I'll be around keeping an eye on the two of you. One last thing to remember is to prepare a plan, visualised it in your mind, feel what you'll be doing, because what's in the brain goes down the rein."

"When you start to walk away with Duke be consistent, squeeze–vibrate those reins, pick up light contact for now, say Walk-on Duke and add a light squeeze, bracing both your lower legs in contact with Duke's rib cage, as he starts to walk, just let your hands move forward with the descent of Duke's head softening your reins, soften the feel of your legs, do not take them right off, just let them be there. If Duke responds to that, fine, if not keep increasing the pressure with your lower legs until he does walk on then, soften. Go ahead and try that."

The girl and Duke did a beautiful Walk-on from where they were standing. It went so smoothly it took the girl completely by surprise.

"Wow that felt so good, Good Boy Duke," said the girl. "That was great. I have never done that before."

"Looking good," said the Ole' Man, "just keep on going, trust him, enjoy the ride home."

"Bye-Bye for now, and thank you so much," said the girl. "Oh! and Duke thanks you too."

The Ole' Man waved and smiled, as he watched them walk away. "Maybe, just maybe," he thought, "they could become a team." He found some shade and sat on a rock continuing to watch them walk away and disappear over the edge of a large sand dune, and then they were gone.

Chapter 9

The Ole' Man leaned his back against the rock face of the out cropping, which towered above him, reaching to the heavens above.

"I suppose many people will continue to follow the old ways," thought the Ole' Man, "getting the same old results, and in some cases still creating problem horses."

He hoped that his work with the girl and Duke, by just suggesting some different ways of doing things, that maybe, just maybe some of the girl's friends, and people at the barn, might start to recognise how happy and comfortable in his work Duke was becoming now. How light in the bridle, responsive and better conditioned he generally was. That maybe they would consider introducing things, just a little differently to their horses. By understanding yet again, that if they needed their horses to change, they themselves would have to change some of the things that they were doing first.

The Ole' Man closed his eyes, exhaled and smiled to himself. Maybe this young lady could be the future – the next generation.

The girl and Duke had a wonderful ride back to the barn, she felt less tense and more confident than she could ever recall. They were so much more together, as one.

Upon reaching the barn, she gave Duke a bath with cool water, he really enjoyed that. Even drinking from the hose as she lightly sprayed his face. Duke received extra hay in his corral, after filling up his water trough with clean fresh water.

The girl watched from the fence, as Duke circled a few times, smelled and pawed at the ground, before dropping to his knees to become involved in some very serious rolling.

The girl went to the barn and finished putting her tack away. She glanced at the clock in the barn and found it hard to believe that only four hours had past since she had left earlier that morning. She was somewhat confused, and unclear as to what had happened. There had been other occasions, when the girl often thought that Duke and she seemed to have learned and accomplished so much. When within the Circle of Knowledge and Truth with the Ole' Man, it had seemed on occasion, that they were almost in another world, one in which time just did not seem to matter that much, or to be the same, somehow.

The girl had some extra *Manifestation Cards* in her tack box, and so she thought, while so much was still fresh in her mind, that she would make some notes, and take one set of cards back home with her.

The next day, as the Ole' Man suggested, was to be a light day of work for both of them. That evening the girl resolved to have an early night, so she could be at the barn bright and early, to take advantage of the cool of the day to work Duke. Then just fit in a nice trail ride to finish off for the day.

Before going to sleep the girl decided to review all of her notes. When she got to the last card covering the most recent work with the Ole' Man, Ideas, thoughts and feelings were dancing in her head. Her thoughts swirled around the many new and exciting experiences she had recently shared with Duke.

The girl also contemplated on the many insights and the wealth of knowledge, the Ole' Man had been kind enough to share with her during their many talks, while giving Duke well-deserved breaks. Her thoughts drifted back to the clock in the barn. Could it be that time really had stood still.

During the deep sleep of the evening, the following was revealed to her. That yes, it was possible within the Circle of Knowledge and Truth that time had stood still, but that by allowing the new energy to flow freely between Duke and her, it helped free them both, leading to an awareness, closeness with each other, becoming as one.

Within all of this, her sense of being able to really have contact with and feel Duke movements helped her to be with him, and not to restrict him or be in his way, and with all of this, her confidence soared.

It seemed they had developed a much deeper level of understanding of each other, leading to operating at a higher level of consciousness. In the dream, the girl could actually see Duke he looked so happy in his work, gone was the previous tension and stress, he learned the movements or new tasks so much more easily now.

Something was now irritating and seemed to be buzzing in her ear. While the girl started to wake up, she found herself somewhere between the encroaching dawn of the reality of a new day, and the birth of the new knowledge within the shadows of her dreams.

Could all of these new experiences be real, she glanced at the clock, seven in the morning, that's fine she thought. She quickly had some breakfast, and packed lunch for while she was away from home for the day. She headed for Duke and the barn, excited at the prospect of working with her horse and seeing if he really had improved in the real world, as much as he was doing in her dreams and thoughts.

On the way to the barn she remembered the Ole' Man had told her that, your thoughts in this moment helped produce your future desired results, or outcome. The girl continued to tell herself that this would be the best day of riding that she and Duke had ever had, that Duke would be excellent.

She focused on these thoughts all the way to the barn. At the same time, as the girl approached Duke's corral, he was over in the far corner grazing. The girl stood by the gate and called out to her horse "Duke Come," as she lifted her right arm above her head. Duke looked up from grazing, his ears focused towards the gate. The girl then made a rapid kissing sound, and Duke started to walk towards her. When he reached the gate, the girl gave him a small piece of apple, and praised him with a stroke on his neck, and said "Good Boy Duke."

The girl offered her halter to Duke, and he lowered his head to receive the halter. Duke was placed in cross ties, groomed and tacked up, the girl fitted her halter on top of her bridle, and made-up her reins safely.

The girl then removed the cross ties, and spent a few minutes asking Duke to lower his head, as she applied pressure to the halter with her lead shank. Duke seemed a little unsure to start with, but the girl had confidence in Duke being able to do it, if she just had the patience, maintained a light contact and waited for Duke to soften. Duke moved his head around a little, and the girl did her best to just follow the movements of Duke's head. Duke soon recognised what was being asked of him, and he softened just a little, to test the girl.

The girl smiled and quickly softened the contact she had, but remembered not to release completely all the contact, and just softened the feel.

The girl praised Duke and tried again, this time Duke lowered his head about eight inches, and got a little stuck there, "Good Boy Duke," said the girl, as she maintained contact at this position. Duke stayed where he was, the girl wondered if she could lower his head further, she applied a little more pressure. Duke lowered his head another six inches, and the girl immediately softened her contact, "Good Boy Duke," and she quickly gave him a small piece of apple as a reward, this got Duke's attention.

The girl walk Duke forward a few steps, and applied light pressure, Duke immediately lowered his head about half way to the ground before stopping, "What a Smart Boy Your Are," said the girl, and then walked Duke to his stall.

The girl repeated the exercise in Duke's stall, rewarded him with small piece of apple, for another excellent attempt at going to the ground with his head. Duke was tied up safely in his stall, while the girl went to her tack box to pick up her latest filled out *Manifestation Cards* and the lunge whip, lunge line and Side Reins. She also wanted to pick up, from the feed room, four buckets that were stored there, today she had a plan for them.

The girl headed for the large outdoor sand arena, found two sticks, one she stuck in the ground at about the middle of the arena and attached her lunge line to it, then she stretched out the lunge line and just like the Ole'

Man, with the other stick drew a circle in the sand. The girl then placed the four buckets on the outside edge of the circle representing 12-3-6-9 o'clock, as on a clock face, these would be her markers.

The girl then took her *Manifestation Cards* and sat in the centre of the circle, and read the information several times. Then she closed her eyes breathed in deeply, relaxing, and visualised Duke with Side Reins on, lunging around her with a beautiful form, responding to her every wish and command. Duke would, on cue, right by a bucket of her choice, trot or stop and then start to canter when asked. He was working happily through all the skills he now had, at a high level of excellence. The girl asked Duke to Whoa at the 12 o'clock bucket, Duke stopped with his front-end right in line with the bucket.

During her moment of silence and stillness, the girl felt a light breeze and suddenly heard a soft voice whispering to her:

"Remember, always before you ride, or work your horse, to define your intention. Then really get in touch with the emotion and the feeling that you experience at that moment. Take ownership and responsibility for that feeling, immerse yourself in it, search within to become more aware and understand it fully."

"It is so important, because the horse, being the intuitive, empathetic authentic creature that he is, will pick up on what is happening within you, what is going on at your gut level. You have a choice, you can go ahead and continue to fool yourself, however you cannot, and will not be able to fool you horse. He will always, always respond accordingly in an honest manner, as he sees fit, to what he deems to be within his best interest."

"Very simply put, he will reflect your present emotional state."

"Therefore, give thought to these things. I am thankful for being emotionally stable, grounded, confident, well-adjusted, calm, relaxed and happy in this moment."

The voice faded away and the girl found herself back in her silence. Then, she opened her eyes, smiled and stood up.

"Now I am ready to work Duke," the girl said out loud to herself, as she walked with confidence to get Duke from his stall. Between the barn and reaching the arena, the girl stopped three times, and asked Duke to lower his head to the ground. Duke complied by going lower each time, and performed the task willingly. He was rewarded with a piece of apple when he reached the centre of the circle; the girl stroked his neck and praised him. Duke looked calm and relaxed ready to go to work.

The girl removed her lead shank and attached her lunge line, while telling Duke she believed that today, he would perform for her on the lunge line, and riding the best he ever had.

Chapter 10

It had now been quite some time since the girl and the Ole' Man been together. Things had improved greatly, for Duke and her, and once again she found herself riding out into the desert, to seek further answers.

Approaching the rock face, the girl already spotted the Ole' Man, and rushing to him, she recounted her recent experiences and how happy she was.

"Do you remember the first time I helped you to work Duke, and I taught Duke to move his hind-end over away from me? Do you remember that," asked the Ole' Man.

"Yes, yes I do. You said it was to exercise Duke's hind-end and help him become focused on you," answered the girl.

"That's right," said the Ole' Man, "it can be used as an exercise to teach a horse how to learn the basics of a lateral work, and working towards the turn on the fore hand. I like to give a horse a really good idea of how to do these movements, while I am here with them on the ground."

"Then, I find when I add a rider to the equation, it all comes together so much easier and faster, and is as stress free as possible for the horse."

"A large part of this whole new approach is to teach the horse, as much as possible from the ground. When the horse is confident and understands what we want from him, there is a natural progression to having a rider on his back, whose main job is not to get in the way of the movement, and to just apply the required aids with his legs and hands."

"I said legs first, because I believe most of our communication with the horse should be about eighty percent legs and seat, and only the rest with our hands."

"It can be a humbling experience, because the horse can already do the movement without you up there. It's just a matter of refinement from there on. What I mean by that is, when you see a horse and rider completing some movements together, you should not be able to see the rider doing anything. In order to get up there, to that level, it makes sense to start the horse down here, on the ground, that's where at this basic level we can help him so much, or if you find you are still having a problem, then dismount and work him through the movement from the ground, lunge him for a few minutes."

"After that, get back on and start again. Give him time to learn, to process, and it goes without saying, lots of praise."

"If I may, let me show you this simple exercise," said the Ole' Man.

With that, the girl handed Duke over to the Ole' Man. The Ole' Man attached his soft rope to Duke's halter, put Duke out on a fifty foot circle lunging him to the left, and then taking him up and down through transitions to warm Duke up and get him focused, ready to learn a new task.

"There's a Good Boy Duke," said the Ole' Man, happy with Duke's warm up, "Whoa Duke, there's a Good Boy."

Duke stopped and looked in towards the Ole' Man, who walked over to him, stood alongside and praised him further, stroked his neck, then led Duke into the centre of the circle.

"Watch for a few minutes, pay attention to how and where Duke places his hind legs, and then when you are riding him, you'll have a greater understanding of what Duke has to do with his legs and feet. For myself, I found it helped me enormously when I became aware of where my horse's feet had to be, before I asked them to try to do a certain movement."

"Let's get started before Duke becomes bored with me talking. I'll try to describe what I am doing, as Duke and I go through this movement," concluded the Ole' Man.

"With my rope about eight feet long in my left hand, and standing in line with your saddle, I'm going to turn my shoulders now and look towards Duke's hip, there."

"I am picking up some contact with my left hand, watch; Duke is now starting to move his front-end. I'm softening my contact, because I am walking towards his left hip and leg, because I want Duke to move away from me, by him stepping with his left leg deep underneath himself and crossing well in front of his right hind leg. Good Boy Duke, there you go."

"Never pull, or have too much contact with his halter. That would cause Duke to put too much weight down through his left shoulder to his foot."

"At this level, he has to be able to walk a small circle around me, as you can see he is doing, as I continue to apply pressure to his hip by walking towards it."

"Now, I'm going to swing about ten inches of the free-end of my rope in my right hand towards his left hip, which Duke can see. I just want to add a little bit more pressure to get him to pay attention and liven up a little."

"Good Boy, a couple of quick steps, there, that's good," praised the Ole' Man.

"Now I have stopped swinging the rope's free-end, which in effect is softening the pressure that I was applying on him. It's still all about pressure, and less pressure, and Duke is learning to respect that, and of course praise and reward."

"What in effect I am doing here, is having Duke move out of my space. Just like another horse might come over to Duke's hip and say move over, but my intention is to use this, as a part of our building block approach to teach the horse an element towards developing a lateral movement."

The Ole' Man praised Duke and then lunged him to the right for a few minutes through some transitions to loosen him up again.

Returning to the centre of the circle with Duke, the Ole' Man explained to the girl the importance of whatever you have done to the left, also to repeat to the right. Now the Ole' Man was going to ask Duke to move his hind-end over to the left side.

"Duke was a little stiffer this way in trying to move his right hind leg under himself in front of his left hind leg. What this tells me is that Duke will need you to work him more going to his left side. That will help move his rib cage over, you'll find that by doing this, it will help riding Duke straight later on in his training," said the Ole' Man.

After working Duke this way, the Ole' Man helped the girl for a few minutes in having Duke completing the exercise both ways.

Duke was coming along nicely and the Ole' Man was pleased with him.

The girl was all smiles and happy with this new movement that her and Duke were now doing. "How does this help with a lateral movement," inquired the girl.

"I am glad you asked," said the Ole' Man. "When you are riding Duke, having the ability to be able to control his hind-end will mean that you can place it where you want to, because Duke will move his hind leg as you request him to do."

"By reaching about four to six inches back from where your girth is let's say right here," the Ole' Man placed the flat of his knuckles against Duke's lower rib cage lightly. "This is where your lower leg would be. Watch and I'll ask Duke to move his hind-end with the knuckles of my left hand placed here, with my right hand applying a little pressure to the halter to free up Duke's feet."

"Here we go, Good Boy Duke, as Duke started to lift his right hind leg, I press with the flat of my knuckles to influence that right hind leg to move under him."

"You can see that when he has completed the stride, I soften my hand. I do not take it completely away, this way it helps Duke to learn, yet again, to distinguish between pressure and less pressure, or an active aid or a passive aid, as my hand is now softly there, on his rib cage, supporting," said the Ole' Man.

"Well, yet again Duke is doing so well, and I have a lot of confidence in Duke being able and willing to do this with me in fact, I consider that we are doing it together."

"I want to move on to the next stage while Duke is still interested."

"Are you still interested," the Ole' Man asked the girl.

"I'd say so," said the girl, "it was really neat how Duke moved over from just your hand being where my leg would have been. I can hardly wait to try to ride that. How long before I can get Duke to do that with me riding him," asked the girl enthusiastically.

"Give me about another fifteen minutes, and you can get back on Duke and ride, what some people call leg yielding. How does that sound to you?"

"That sounds great, I can hardly wait," said the girl.

"My expectation would be that Duke will be able to at least give you three strides, as a basic to leg yielding. This will get you started on this, and it will be up to you to continue to use this exercise, as a foundation to refine this movement. Let's get started, I'll lunge Duke to the left to warm him up again," said the Ole' Man.

The Ole' Man put Duke through transitions for a few minutes, and then brought him back into the centre of the circle, and spent a few minutes having Duke step over with his left leg. Duke was by now doing this really well with confidence and in a relaxed frame of mind. The Ole' Man was happy with Duke's progress, and was now going to prepare Duke to walk a couple of strides of the leg yielding from the ground.

"Good Boy, Duke," said the Ole' Man, stroking his neck just after Duke had completed his last step over with his left hind leg.

"I'll do my best to explain what I am doing, please watch Duke's hind legs and his front legs, because during this movement sideways, Duke will be crossing his front left leg over and in front of his right leg."

"You see that rock face at the edge of our circle in the sand, I'm going to use that to help Duke's forward motion into a sideways movement. When you ride this at home, you'll be able to use the fence line to assist you. Later on, as Duke progresses in his level of training with the leg yielding, you'll move further and further away from the fence and eventually, you'll be able to ride Duke's leg yielding wherever you want to in your arena."

"Watch now I'm going to walk Duke in a couple of medium-sized circles, building forward motion, I want energy in this walk, Duke needs to be alive, fluid, forward and focused on what we are doing."

"When I come off the top of the circle, as you can see, I'm leading Duke with my right hand about halfway down the lead shank, walking briskly towards the rock face now approaching it at about forty five degrees, quickly I turn to face Duke's side and now place my left hand on the lead shank, about eight inches below his jaw, to help place his head in the direction of travel."

"I have now placed my right hand about eight inches away from the end of my lead shank. On this first attempt I am lightly flicking the free-end of my lead shank against Duke's side, right where your leg will be just behind your girth, which is about four to six inches. This will help influence Duke to step sideways away from me, as I step towards the centre of his rib cage with focused energy."

Duke took a couple of steps away from the Ole' Man, and got his feet a little stuck in the ground. The Ole' Man however was thrilled with the amount of effort that Duke had displayed.

"What a Good Boy Duke, you did really well," said the Ole' Man, then he stroked Duke's neck and gave him a small piece of apple.

The girl was happy and very surprised to see Duke crossing front and hind legs together, while moving sideways on an angle to the rock face.

"There," said the Ole' Man, "that's a good start I'm going to establish a high energy brisk walk again, I'll be here at his left shoulder as usual. Watch again, while I make the switch to my left hand, as I turnaround to face Duke's left side. Here I go, as I reach the rock face, and I step towards Duke's left side this time, I am placing the flat of my knuckles of my right hand right here, just where your lower leg would be."

Applying pressure each time, Duke's left hind leg comes off the ground, "Good Boy, Good Boy Duke, well done." The Ole' Man praised him.

"This is going really well," said the Ole' Man, "in part, you must remember, it's because Duke has the skills and the conditioning in place, before attempting this movement."

"So what do you think so far, can you see how this can help Duke and you, in presenting to Duke the foundation of a new movement for him to learn," asked the Ole' Man.

The girl was stroking Duke's neck and also praising him, "what a smart boy you are Duke," she said, "Yes, I am so impressed, it really does help me to understand, as you teach Duke from the ground, and I am becoming more aware of where Duke's feet need to be to complete the movement."

"I also realise that Duke will have a really good understanding of how to do this movement before I get on. Then, with your help in guiding me where to place my hands and legs to help Duke, I can see this way is a lot faster and easier for the horse. In fact Duke can already do it, I just have to learn how to become a part of the movement with him," said the girl.

"That's correct," Complimented the Ole' Man, "so often people are trying to teach something from the saddle, and can give so many wrong signals to the horse. In the beginning, the horse has too much to try to focused on, that he becomes confused, maybe even afraid. Then mentally and emotionally you have lost the window of opportunity to try to teach him anything."

To make sure that Duke fully understood this movement, the Ole' Man continued to work with him slowly and consistently through four more passes in front of the rock face. Sometimes, Duke actually went through three and four complete strides quite well.

The Ole' Man went on to explain, that you could see that Duke was really trying and was calm and relaxed, yet focused on his work. That Duke was not stressed and was having a good experience. In fact he was always being set up for success, which in itself is an empowering process.

"It's important to realise that Duke should be, as happy and as relaxed at the end of our teaching him something new, as he was at the beginning of our work session."

The Ole' Man was happy with Duke's performance from the ground, and was now confident that Duke was well prepared to move to the next stage, ready to accept and try to perform the lateral movement with the rider on-board.

With this in mind, he turned to the girl and suggested that it was time for her to ride Duke. While the Ole' Man stood by Duke's side in the centre of the circle, the girl was only too eager to mount and get back on Duke and ride this new lateral movement.

"Before you actually ride Duke through this movement, let me take a few minutes to give you the required instructions you'll need to help Duke," said the Ole' Man.

"For the first couple of tries I'm going to walk with you and Duke, to help you both and be supportive, and then you'll continue to ride by yourself. There are two key points for you to focus on, to help support Duke through this movement."

"Like always, let's start with your legs. Duke is going to be traveling to his right, so as you saw from the ground, his left hind leg will be the one to step toward the centre of his body in front of his right hind leg," pointed out the Ole' Man.

"When his left hind-foot comes off the ground I'm going to help you by saying *now*."

"At that point, four to six inches behind your girth, with your lower leg, I'll need you to apply pressure, as if to sweep Duke's left leg underneath him."

"At this stage of training, your right leg can be straight underneath you, passive, supporting. Later on in the development of this movement, it will become more active, in asking the horse to have a forward motion, or control Duke's hind-end if he should try to move more to the right."

"Your right hand is most important. You'll need the required amount of contact to stop Duke from trying to bend his head back to his left. For now you can try to have Duke's nose pointing a little to the right, as you continue to be supportive with the contact of your left rein."

"This all helps keep Duke's head, neck and shoulders in line, where you need them. It is a balancing act, as you keep him between your hands and legs. That's about as simple as I can make it at this level, I hope I am helping to make it easy and clear to understand," said the Ole' Man.

"Remember, you do know that Duke can do this, trust and have faith in him. One last thing, stay relaxed, breathe and look slightly to the right with your eyes, it always helps to look in the direction you're traveling. Are you ready to ride this, do you have any questions," asked the Ole' Man.

"I think that's pretty well clear to me, and Duke can do it quite well. I am ready to do my best. It would be great, if you'll just walk through it with me for a couple of times, to get us started," answered the girl.

"Of course," the Ole' Man assured her, "let's get started by walking on a couple of circles to get Duke moving again. Apply more of the driving seat, and equally apply little more pressure with both of your lower legs, to tell Duke to liven up his walk, to move forward and be in front of your legs. We want to do this, to build more energy into the forward motion, so it will be there when we need it to be converted into the required power to become a lateral movement."

They walked a few more circles together, discussed a few more finer points, building the energy, preparing themselves for the first pass in front of the sheer rock face at the edge of their circle.

"Visualise the energy flowing forward; let's start towards the rock face. Look, remember to look a little to your right, keep breathing. Slightly turn your shoulders to the right, in line with Duke's shoulders, good."

The Ole' Man had now turned from leading Duke to facing the girl's left leg, and helping encourage Duke to take that all-important first step.

"Now," said the Ole' Man, "as Duke's left hind leg just started to lift off the ground, apply your left leg, sweep Duke's left leg under him."

"A little more contact with your right rein," instructed the Ole' Man.

"Now again in time with Duke's left leg, try to feel it," suggested the Ole' Man.

"One more time, now."

"Well done, Good Boy Duke that was marvellous. I am so proud of both of you, that was excellent. It really does help to demonstrate how important laying a solid foundation in preparation to doing these movements is to the horse, and keeping stress levels down and setting him up for success." The Ole' Man was indeed very happy with their progress.

Duke had taken, at their first attempt three complete strides of this in part sideways, lateral movement.

"How did that feel," inquired the Ole' Man.

"Absolutely amazing, I am thrilled, it felt so good," exclaimed the girl, "I could tell Duke was really trying, he felt pretty solid underneath me. Could we please try a couple more, so I can get a really good feel and understanding of what we are doing?"

"Yes that's what I had in mind. Let's keep moving, so we make sure we keep Duke interested and motivated."

The Ole' Man continued to walk with Duke and the girl for two more complete leg yielding movements along the rock face.

Duke continued to do well, and completed three strides each time. The Ole' Man now thought it was time to remove his rope from Duke's halter. He explained that he would walk with them for the next movement, to carry on being supportive.

Then, at the next circle, he would remain in the middle of the circle and give instructions only as required.

When the girl came around to start the movement, the Ole' Man stood facing the girl's left leg and lifted up both arms with the palms of his hand facing Duke's side, he walked towards Duke helping the girl to continue the lateral movement.

Duke made four complete strides, and as a result, Duke received a piece of apple and much praise from both of them.

The girl started to ride another circle and started to find her way back to the now familiar rock face. The Ole' Man eased himself away from them and found the centre of the circle.

On the first pass, he offered only the occasional, "now," as the hind leg came off the ground, and, "just a little more contact with your right rein." It was time for Duke and the girl to get a feel for each other, as they worked their way through the next three passes.

On the last attempt Duke and the girl completed five strides before they got a little stuck.

"I'm almost lost for words, you and Duke are outstanding. It just does not get any better than that. Let's give Duke a treat and a well-deserved break. Maybe dismount for a few minutes and let's sit in the shade." Suggested the

Ole' Man.

The three of them walked over and found shade within the now familiar confines of the towering sheer rock face, at the edge of the Circle of Knowledge and Truth.

Duke received a couple of pieces of apple, as a well-deserved treat, much praise and a chance to rest.

"Let's go over here and sit in the shade, let's have a little chat while we allow Duke to process this last session," said the Ole' Man.

Chapter 11

"Duke is doing so well. He's really coming along nicely. All the lunging, conditioning work with the Side Reins that you have been doing has been helping Duke enormously. Duke has started to develop softness in the lower jaw, by understanding the concept of softening to light pressure from the bit," complimented the Ole' Man.

"While we are here today, how about if I take the opportunity to share with you and Duke how to perform the movement called Rein-Back," asked the Ole' Man.

"I believe in teaching the rein-back to horses, or as some people say backup, as early as possible. Are you interested," asked the Ole' Man.

The girl laughed, "I cannot backup Duke, and many of my friends, who have some horses that are eight to ten years old, and have been riding them for years, cannot back their horses up."

"That's interesting," said the Ole' Man, "can you describe what happens generally with your friends' horses?"

The girl made a bit of a funny face. "Most of my friends just seem to pull back with both reins. The horses often poke their noses forward and lift up their heads and neck; some do not move at all, it's just a pulling competition. Others, hollow their back, step sideways and go crooked. I think that's about the way it goes. Oh! And yes, I remember one girl's horse rearing at one time, that looked scary."

Looking at the ground, the Ole' Man shook his head. "Let's take a different approach," said the Ole' Man, "because it would seem that the results they were getting would not be the result that we want, or Duke for that matter."

"I am going to describe how Duke will be able, in a reasonable given timeframe, to be capable of performing a beautiful backup for you."

"Are you ready and receptive to the new information?"

"Sounds interesting," said the girl, "I'm ready."

"I want you to just sit there quietly, absolutely relaxed, breathing deeply, as I describe Duke going through how he will eventually perform a flawless backup. I want you to be focused in your mind, and really in this whole movement with Duke, not only seeing it, but feeling the complete new experience of the backup, or rein-back."

"I'm just going to talk you through it, this is what we call starting with the end-result in mind, in this case it's Duke backing up for you, But it does work well with other things too."

"Right then," said the Ole' Man. "Here we go, feel this, Duke has come to a collected stop, halt, he is soft and light equally in both hands, awaiting further instructions from you, because he is in a collected frame his head is almost vertical to the ground, he stopped square with his front feet, and they are in line with each other, evenly weighted and well placed under his shoulders. The back is lifted up rounded, you can actually feel Duke's back filling your seat, it's like he's lifting you up. His croup is a little lowered; his hind legs are square and balanced with even weight on each foot standing naturally underneath him."

"He is well positioned in this powerful frame ready to go anywhere, and do anything you wish. Your legs are placed at the girth; they are passive and supporting just being there ready to speak to Duke."

"Now, I want you to vibrate your reins and squeeze them, make them come alive in your hands, which will then gently speak to Duke's mouth. Your hands are going to remain where they are, then with your lower leg you are going to apply more pressure to Duke's lower rib cage by closing your legs, because your hands do not move Duke will not go forward, he will respect the light contact and start to backup. His smooth two beat diagonal gait carries you straight back, equally between your hands, also your shoulders are square to his shoulders, your hips are square to his hips, you are in balance and in complete harmony with each other."

"You maintain supportive light contact with the bit, Duke's head and neck remains straight in line with his shoulders."

"You maintain the same degree of contact with your legs, after four strides back you softened your legs, but you do not take them completely off Duke, again they are now passive just there lightly resting against his sides. Duke then just simply halts, stops, awaiting further instructions."

"You reward him by remaining passive in your seat and legs, you are in neutral, you slowly move your hands forward and down towards his withers, place your reins in one hand put your hand on his withers and with the other hand reach forward to stroke Duke's neck and praise him verbally."

"I think you should open your eyes now, Duke was outstanding could you feel that, could you imagine you and Duke going through the effortless rein-back or backup?"

"Yes. I could see Duke, and I was doing that. I could feel us moving together. I would love to be able to do that, would you help me understand how to achieve that level of excellence," said the girl.

The Ole' Man, smiling, said, "I thought you might like to backup like that, it will take you some time to achieve that level. But I think we can agree that you have the end-result in mind, and that's the most important first step. The second is for you to believe and have the faith that you can do it. Are you willing to practice it?"

"Yes, would it be possible to get started on it right now, and then I could continue to practice during the next few days."

The Ole' Man had to explain further. "Within the next ten minutes you'll be back on him, and I'm sure Duke will at least take some steps back with you. Ten minutes of ground work will again save you a lot of time; this is the easy and quick way."

The girl, respecting all that the Ole' Man had been able to share with her so far, was quick to say, "How do I teach Duke to backup from here?"

"Now, Because Duke is soft in the jaw, and has a well conditioned hind-end, it will be a lot easier to teach him to backup, just let me show you how to do this, then you can try a couple of times yourself and then we will move on to the next part," said the Ole' Man.

With that, the Ole' Man positioned himself to the left and in front of Duke, but to the side and facing Duke's left shoulder, with the lead shank in his right hand about six inches below the jaw, the remainder of the lead shank was in his left hand. The Ole' Man slightly turned his right shoulder, and pointed slightly at Duke's left shoulder.

"The backup is a two beat diagonal gait, which means the opposite front and hind leg move back together as one stride. Take a look at Duke's front leg, as he is standing now his left front leg is well ahead of his right, which means his right front leg is now carrying most of Duke's body weight."

"I am now moving Duke's head, so it comes over towards his left leg, there's a Good Boy, now I'm going to apply pressure directly with my right hand, and project my energy diagonally straight through his left shoulder, across his back to his right hind leg, and down through his hock to his right hind foot. Imagine you are shooting an arrow full of energy right to that right hind foot, which causes Duke to take a step back," the Ole' Man then took a step forward with his left right towards Duke's left front leg."

The girl watched in amazement, as the Ole' Man rocked Duke back and forth and in time with the stepping sequence of Duke's front leg, as he applied the request to backup.

Following the Ole' Man stepping forward with his right leg, Duke would step back moving his left front and right hind legs, the Ole' Man would then step back and Duke would follow. It was like a dance, the Ole' Man then moved over to Duke's right shoulder and repeated the dance routine.

The Ole' Man walked Duke for a couple of circles, and then came back to the same place and praised Duke. Duke looked completely happy and relaxed, focused on the Ole' Man.

"Good Boy Duke," and reaching into his pocket he gave Duke a small piece of apple and then stroked Duke's neck, "Good Boy."

"Duke is ready now to take a couple of steps back, I'll only have to move his head slightly from side to side, because he understands now simply to back off of the pressure and when he does, he softens, and of course, I soften, as soon as I can feel the difference."

"I do not let go completely, I become passive with my hand, then I apply pressure again for the next stride, so pressure – I feel a response from Duke, even a try is rewarded by lessening in the pressure, becoming soft and supporting."

"That's the difference, that's the reward we want him to seek, or search for in many things we teach him to do. The horse can understand that concept when applied consistently, and always followed by an instant reward of some kind."

"They want, need and deserve that from us, consistently," the Ole' Man stressed this important point.

The Ole' Man walked a circle again with Duke, had him stop, moved in front of Duke and simply stepped towards Duke with confidence saying "Duke back, Good Boy. He had Duke complete four strides back, stop, and then the Ole' Man moved to Duke's shoulder reached up with his right hand stroked his neck and praised him, "Duke, well done."

Turning to the girl, the Ole' Man inquired, "So what do you think, that just took a few minutes and Duke is really getting the idea."

"I'll say," said the girl, "Duke's doing so well you were right, it's interesting to understand how the horse has to move his feet, so can I try couple of times with Duke."

"Well that's exactly what I had in mind," said the Ole' Man. "I know you can do it and you know Duke can do it, so let's put it all together."

"Then we will move on to the next part, and that will help keep it interesting for Duke."

The Ole' Man handed the lead shank to the girl, she positioned herself in front of Duke just like the Ole' Man, at first when she applied pressure to the halter, Duke was a bit stuck and started to move his head up and down.

"Stay with him," suggested the Ole' Man, "just be patient, keep contact with him, really get a feel of the contact with him, I think maybe you have a bit too much pressure on him, just soften a little, give him a chance to find you."

"Now, move his head a little more over his shoulder, and apply a little more diagonal pressure, and see it flowing right through to Duke's hind foot, then he will move it."

Duke eased up and took one step back. The girl smiled and remembered to soften her contact.

"Great," said the Ole' Man, "move his head to the other shoulder and get one more stride."

The girl moved Duke's head over.

"Apply a little more pressure, good, say Duke Back, be determined he will pick up on that feeling from you, after he completes that step, stand straight in front of him, straighten his head, apply just the right amount of pressure and say Duke Back, Good Boy, step towards him to move him with each stride."

The Ole' Man was getting excited, as he saw Duke continue to take steps back in time to the girl's wishes.

"Wow," said the girl, he did it, he did it, he took four steps back, "Good Boy Duke, Good Boy."

The Ole' Man was stroking Duke's neck, "Well done Duke Good Boy," and gave him another piece of apple, as a treat.

"Do you think I could now actually ride him for four steps in backup, I think we're both ready for it," said the girl.

"Well, of course," said the Ole' Man, "I thought you would never ask. Let's go on to the next stage, up you get."

Once mounted and settled, the girl was all smiles, she had picked up her reins and had Duke on light contact. Her legs were just lightly against Duke's sides. Both were relaxed and ready to do a nice backup, rein-back of four strides.

"I want you to sit for a few minutes and breathe, close your eyes, and go through the beautiful backup that I described to you before, remember? I want you to feel and believe Duke and you can do this," said the Ole' Man.

"Yes, said the girl, and I do believe Duke can do this, he is well prepared and ready, and so am I."

While the girl sat there, the Ole' Man stood in front of Duke with the lead shank still on Duke's halter.

"Are you ready," said the Ole' Man.

"Yes, very," answered the girl.

"We are just going to walk Duke around in a large circle, because he has been just standing here for a few minutes, just to get his legs moving and help refocus him. When we get back to the same spot I am going to ask you to watch Duke, I'll then stand directly in front of him."

"You have two main things to focus on when we ask Duke, you'll support him to backup on light contact through your reins, you'll not, under any circumstances, pull back on the reins, and you cannot let Duke pull your hands forward."

"Next, your legs will close on his rib cage. After four steps, soften your legs, but keep them on his sides and sit a little heavier in your seat. When he stops, maintain the same contact with his face for a moment or two, have him there nice and soft, steady him so that he is not pulling or fussing around with his face at all, then you'll move your hands forward down and towards his withers. Lighten your seat and stroke his neck and praise him. I hope I am making myself clear."

"Yes," said the girl.

By the time the Ole' Man had explained this to the girl they had made a large circle and were back to the place they had started from. Duke had stopped with his front left foot out ahead of his right.

The Ole' Man quickly moved in front of Duke, in line with Duke's left shoulder.

"Pick up that light contact on both sides of Duke's bit," the Ole' Man said to the girl, "do you feel that?"

"Yes," said the girl

"Good," said the Ole' Man.

"Do remember, do not let Duke pull your hands out of position, they must convey to him 'No Duke! You cannot go forward'."

"Now, I'll be here to help, if needed."

"I want you now to apply pressure with your legs, go head."

Duke did fuss a little with his head, but the girl followed his head to maintain contact that would stop him from going forward. She soon had him settled and on the bit.

"Ask again with your legs, and say Duke Back," said the Ole' Man.

Duke took his first step back, "ask again with your legs, equally," said the Ole' Man, "try to ask with each stride," Duke took another step, "again," said the Ole' Man. This continued, and Duke completed four steps of backup with a rider for the first time ever.

The girl softened her aids, stroked Duke's neck and continued to praise him, she was so proud of him.

The Ole' Man was thrilled that it had gone so well for both of them. He gave Duke another small piece of apple, and then said to the girl, "well done, you did extremely well, I'm very proud of you, you are really developing a feel and timing, and those two things are so important to develop, as skills."

"The next stage is," said the Ole' Man, "of course, for you and Duke to backup by yourselves. At this level of training Duke will quite likely stop with one front foot forward slightly ahead of the other. With time, we can square up his halt, stop stand, but you can use it now to your advantage to help to continue improving the backup, or rein-back."

"Remember this is the key, the foot that is ahead has less weight on it, and that will always be the foot that has to take the first step back."

"To continue, this is what you can do. When Duke stops, look over his front-end to see which foot is forward, you can also watch the placement of his shoulders indicating which foot is forward."

"Let's assume that Duke stops for you with his left foot forward well ahead of his right, and then you are going to help that left foot take the first step back by using your left hand in a slightly curling motion from your wrist, as you apply your legs, as usual try to feel each stride watching the shoulders. To start with, it can help you to feel Duke's hip and hind leg, move as it gets lifted up into your seat, apply your legs equally with each stride to keep him straight, squeezing and softening."

"Walk Duke around for a couple of circles to loosen him up, and get him refocused and at the same time, play your how to do this plan in your mind. When you're ready, return to this spot and check for that front foot. Then ride each stride to an excellent backup, I know you can do it. Make sure you keep breathing and remain relaxed and confident, Duke will pick up on that from you."

The girl walked Duke for a few more large circles and returned to the same spot, and asked Duke to Whoa. Duke stopped with his left front foot forward. The girl maintained, as best she could, the light contact on Duke's bit, as Duke's head descended into her hands for the stop, halt.

"Good," said the Ole' Man, standing off to one side.

"Just spend a moment and breathe, relax and give Duke time to settle. Can you feel both sides of the bit?"

"When you are ready, squeeze your reins, make them come alive, which will help Duke come to life. Next, support him with your right rein, as you curl your left wrist, which will give you the required contact with your left side of Duke's face. This will help encourage him to move that left front foot back, apply your legs with each stride."

The girl smoothly applied these aids to Duke, and because of Duke's level of conditioning, and all the time that had been taken in preparing him step by step to understand the concept of the backup, Duke backed up remarkably well, he made three complete steps and got a little stuck there. This was an excellent first attempt and everyone was pleased, including Duke.

"That's great, excellent," almost shouting with excitement, exclaimed the Ole' Man. "Let's stop there, start to soften your aids to reward him, legs should be passive, seat becoming lighter, hands moving forward and down towards the withers, that lets him stretch his head and neck, place your reins in one hand, reach for his neck and withers, stroke him and praise him, well done."

"Are you happy with that, what did it feel like, it looked good to me from where I was standing," asked the Ole' Man.

The girl was extremely happy and it showed all over her face. Looking at the Ole' Man she said "Duke was so kind, most of the time he felt nice and soft in his face, he did push against my hands a couple of times, but nothing too bad or hard. I was able to keep my hands stable quite easily and I could feel him soften, it felt great generally, and I could feel Duke moving under me."

"Well done both of you," said the Ole' Man, "I think you and Duke have done lots for now, maybe you would like to dismount and I suggest we give Duke a treat. Let's sit in the shade over there for a few minutes, before you have to head for home."

The three of them found a cool place to rest amidst the towering rock face, at the edge of the Circle of Knowledge and Truth in the sand.

"Let's take a few minutes and discuss something that is very important. I want to try to share with you what happens when Duke is moving forward for you."

"There is going to be a full flow of energy being transmitted from the engagement of the hind-end producing waves of energy right through the horse's back, which you'll receive as softly as possible into your supporting giving hands, allowing it to flow through, so you can receive the next wave."

"That sounds exciting," said the girl, "but I have no idea how to do that."

"It's easy," said the Ole' Man. "I am going to give you a concept that you can tap into, and meditate on when you are not riding. Then later on, you'll use these techniques to help improve your feel when you're riding Duke."

"I would like you to imagine that you are standing on the beach, the waves are coming from behind you, your knees are slightly bent, you reach down with your hands into the wave of water, fingers slightly open, wrists soft and giving. The wave touches your seat, you rise with it, the wave gently passes through your fingers, and you are ready to receive the next wave, you ride the wave, in harmony with the natural energy source. All is fluid soft and flowing, you are a part of the never-ending cycle of energy, there is unity and harmony, and you become one with it. It requires and asks nothing of you, except from opening yourself up to it, and receive all it has to offer you."

"Let me explain what the opposite will be. Let's return to the crouched position in the water, in a more fixed position with stiffness, tension, no yielding, un-giving fingers and tight wrists. Feel the wave crashing into you, disturbing your balance, you twist and bend fighting to keep your fixed position. The water crashes into your closed unyielding hands, you can see and feel the energy being distributed, shattered in a thousand directions. Before you know it, the next wave is upon you, you loose it; it's chaos."

"What I want you to understand is that this is what is happening when we are pulling on our horse's face; when he is trying his best to give us waves of energy to utilize, to flow forward, when there is no resistance from us being in the way. It is far better to be fluid and ride the wave as one, you actually end up doing less, and yet achieving more."

The Ole' Man sat with his back resting against the backdrop of the rock face, his cream panama hat was pulled down over his eyes. He sat quietly for a few minutes gathering his thoughts, while the sheer rock face towering above them extended cool shadows across the warm desert sand.

He reached down to the Earth and with his index finger he drew a circle in the sand.

"For me, horses are one of The Creator's most noble creatures. At the same time, one of the most honest and forgiving, they are indeed a gift to humanity."

"Horses, I believe, can sense and see through to the core of your soul, of your very being. They become a reflection of your Authentic Self. Try as you may, you cannot fool them, they intuit through all the nonsense. I am sure at times you may play games and fool your friends, but you'll never be able to fool Duke."

"Remember this, and write it out on your *Manifestation Cards*, as soon as you can."

"Horses will never lie to you, and they have no hidden agendas."

The girl laughed, and said she would make a note of it when she got home. The Ole' Man drew a deep breath and continued.

"Around the world there are some great horse teachers, they do not whisper to horses. These people allow the horses to become their greatest teachers. With empathy and a deep and abiding respect for the horse, they build a foundation of mutual respect. Then Bonding takes place, from which the relationship can grow, they become a part of each other's world, they choose to become as one."

Now sounding rather serious the Ole' Man bent over and with his finger he drew another circle within his first circle, and drew a large T in it.

"Now, to truly be able to develop that level of relationship with the horse means, that we all have a choice to make."

"What do you mean, I have a choice to make," inquired the girl.

"Well, let me try to explain," said the Ole' Man.

"If there's one constant thread running through life, it would be defined as change. Let's keep it simple, change may come in the form of something improving or declining. When we first met, things between you and Duke…"

The girl was quick to jump in, "I get it, things were declining, and I had a choice to make, to try to change the state of the relationship."

"That's right," said the Ole' Man, "I am so proud of you!"

"Let's move on. To have that great relationship with your horse that you wanted, you have to be prepared to strip away all the nonsense, the ego and the pretences."

"You have to choose to change, to grow, to be an honest, loving and forgiving, emotionally healthy human being. To be living in the moment, and constantly trying your best to live in the Truth."

"Seeking the truth, will set you free," stressed the Ole' Man.

"Making positive changes leads to personal growth, which should become a constant process of evolving to a higher level of consciousness."

"I do want to share this information with you, and I do realise that it might seem a little difficult right now, but do not worry. It's all pretty straightforward, when you have the guidelines of how to achieve that which you desire. I'll lay it out for you in more detail, some other time."

"That would be great," said the girl.

"Good, learn to recognise that a lot of people are not so interested in change and personal growth, so their only choice is to continue in the blame game. Instead of considering their own possible short comings, they find it easier to say I have a problem horse or friend, when really, for most of the time, the true cause of their manifested problem, lies deep within themselves. Hence you see, it's so important for you to be receptive to changing your mind and thoughts, searching for that inner Truth."

"All of this change comes from within, in order to be able to change all that is around you. For example, Duke has changed by responding to all the wonderful changes that you have had the courage to make in yourself."

"Wouldn't you agree," asked the Ole' Man.

"Oh yes," said the girl. "Duke has changed so much, it's really different from the way it was. Often I feel Duke, in his own way, is trying to help me."

"Let me see," said the Ole' Man reaching down to touch what he also called the Circle of Knowledge and Truth, which he deemed to be a Holy ground. "These are available for all, who wished to travel into the realms of what I call – Spiritual Growth."

"We are all on a journey to find our true selves. Now, some of us take longer than others, and that's OK. Sometimes there are detours going down the wrong road, getting lost in the wrong job, or getting involved in the not-so-healthy relationship."

"During those times of confusion, we tend to make poor choices, which often cause us pain that can come in many forms physical, financial, emotional, and even spiritual. It's all about balance."

"At the core of this balance there are Universal Truths."

"I am sharing this with you, so that, hopefully, you'll realise that if you always just do your best, to have the most pure thoughts you possibly can have, that you stand a good chance to minimize the pain in your life, by making the best healthy choices at all times."

"You can always simply test the power of your thought by asking yourself, is this true, and, will it cause myself or anyone else any harm? Then go ahead and take action accordingly, review the responses and feelings that you have, and then ask is this true?"

"We are so fortunate in having our horses available to us as guides throughout this process, if we would just be receptive enough to be aware and listen to their responses. Consider the feedback we are receiving, then make some adjustments and move on. So working with our horses can become an empowering journey of self discovery and personal growth."

"It will always require of you courage and discipline, it's not ever going to be easy. At times, it will range from being uncomfortable to painful, but the rewards are far reaching and will lead you to a greater understanding of your Authentic Self and Personal Freedom."

The sun was starting its usual descent, and the length of the shadows were now laying like outstretched bare arms across the desert floor, declaring that the night would soon follow.

It was again time for Duke and the girl to start on their journey home. The girl thanked the Ole' Man for sharing so much with her.

"Just before I leave, I would like to ask one thing, you mentioned Authentic Self, what would that be?"

"That's a great question," said the Ole' Man. "I am glad you asked, it's getting late, so I'll tell you as quickly as I can."

"It's very simple really; it's the core or essence of your very soul, the purity of who you were born to be. It's who you really are inside, when you take away all the nonsense, that's all the other stuff a lot of other people have supplied you with, actually to cover up what is the true you."

"Remember I said we are all on a journey," asked the Ole' Man.

"Yes," said the girl.

"Well we are all here for different reasons, the journey is to rediscover and reclaim the purity of your soul."

"Then, discover your mission, and passion in life and work on that."

"Recognizing your Authentic Self is like allowing the genius within you to flow out, to be in harmony with your gifts, so you can do your work, while you are here, to your fullest, and within The Creator's plan for you."

"Only you alone can do this work."

"That's why, it's so important to be in contact with whom you truly are, your Authentic Self."

"I know this seems like a lot of information, but I know you realise that while we were working with Duke, it was true that you had to learn some new knowledge and actual riding skills, but so much of the work has been about you changing worn-out old scripts and outdated belief systems, and replacing them with new insights, developing new thoughts, which have led to empowering experiences that you can continue to build on."

"Being courageous enough to explore personal growth, leads you closer and closer to discovering your Authentic Self."

"It may not be fully clear to you as yet, but you have made great progress, and if you want to, I'll try to guide you a little further, fill in your *Manifestation Cards* out at home, study and meditate on them for a few more days."

"I'll be available if needed; you and Duke will know when the time is right."

"During the next couple of days, continue with all you have been doing, the lunging and trail riding for conditioning, keep up the good work, also from the ground, practice for a few minutes each day the backup, as we have been doing here. Then mount and try it, it should be fine, Duke seems to be pretty comfortable with it."

"You have lots to do for a while. Now, I think you should get Duke back to the barn for a well deserved feed of hay and water, and I would suggest that you'll give him a well deserved day off tomorrow."

"You have to know when to stop working with a horse, so you keep him fresh and interested. I find it really helps to do that with horses, it seems that what we sometimes think is the slow way, is in fact really the fast way."

"You should be very happy and proud of what you and Duke

have been able to accomplish together. You really are doing extremely well, and becoming quite the team, and remember, there is no I in a team. Any comments, concerns or thoughts before you head home today?"

"I am so happy, and yes, I'm very proud of Duke, he really was trying to be with me. I could feel at times I was a little behind in my timing and yet he made the stride. It really helps a lot that the horse can already do the movement really quite well without the rider. In the past, I have seen friends try this movement, and it became nothing but a fight," said the girl.

"Doing this movement this way, first from the ground, meant that things will go so well," agreed the Ole' Man.

"I'll give him a break tomorrow, but I can hardly wait until I can try to ride this movement again. Do you think, when I try, that I should start him from the ground as you did, just to warm him up," wondered the girl.

"That's a good question. Continue lunging with the Side Reins to warm him up. Then, yes, lead him through it from the ground a couple of times, but he will let you know that he is ready. You should then start to ride him through the movement with confidence."

"A couple of good-quality strides to start with, and then continue to build from there, as you keep returning to the same place on your fence line, ride circles in between the movement, do not ask too much of him at first, just keep building on day by day."

"Take him out on some trail rides to keep him fresh and, of course, do not forget lots of praise. Does that help and give you a little bit of an outline for now," asked the Ole' Man.

"Thanks so much, that's a great help, tonight I'll make some notes on my *Manifestation Cards*, so I can continued to meditate and visualise these movements. I really had better get going, we have done so much it must be getting quite late."

"Do not worry I'll be around to help you if and when you should need it," the Ole' Man reassured her.

"You must be on your way, I'll say good bye for now."

The girl and Duke said thanks again and headed out on their journey home.

The Ole' Man just continued to sit on the rock, still in the shade and with great satisfaction, he watched them ride away until they were out of sight.

Chapter 12

The Next day, as the girl walked down the laneway to the farm, she could see over to the corral, that Duke called his home, away from his stall. The fence line prevented her at first from seeing him, and then she noticed he was lying flat out on his side with all four legs stretched out. Her heart raced, as she thought the worst, something was wrong with him, she had never known Duke to be down like this.

Quickly she reached the gate to the corral and called out, "Duke, what are you doing?" Duke lifted up his head and neck in the general direction of the gate to see what was making the noise.

The girl, somewhat relieved, dropped her knapsack by the gate, quickly took a couple of pieces of apple from one of the outer pockets, and was quickly through the gate and on her way over to Duke.

Duke had laid back down again, his legs appeared to go stiff now and he arched his back, as the girl got closer, he folded them under himself to partly sit up, his front legs were now bent at the knees and somewhat under his chest.

"Duke you frightened me, I thought you might be sick," said the girl.

Duke turned his head to face the girl, as she approached his shoulder, and nickered to her, but did not get to his feet; he just sat there on his haunches like a rather large dog.

The girl, standing by his shoulder, thought for a moment that horses generally are known to have an inborn fear of anything being above them, something to do with mountain lions of a bygone age. She then smiled to herself, and thought "Duke must trust me to just remain as he was. Maybe this means a deepening of our relationship, Duke must have more confidence in me now."

She bent over to stroke Duke's neck, he liked that. The girl knelt down beside him and offered him one of the pieces of apple she had with her. Duke wrapped his head and neck around her to take it. He closed his eyes in sheer joy, as he relished the treat. Duke still had not attempted to get to his feet, the girl stroked his withers. "Good Boy Duke, how about another piece of apple?"

The moment Duke had finished the second treat, he turned his head. The girl moved now to her knees to be slightly in front and to the side of Duke, she was at eye level with him. The girl was captivated, as she looked deep into the large soft liquid pools of Duke's eyes, for the first time as never before, she felt like she was almost engulfed by them.

Then the strangest of things happened. While looking into Duke's eyes, his ears were locked onto her, and she heard quite clearly and softly:

"Be not afraid, I am here with you."

"Maybe, for the first time in your life you can hear me, your horse. I know so much more than you realise, listen, I can do it all without you. Just open up your heart and soul to me, really *hear* what I am often trying to tell you. Be receptive to the messages and my body language, listen and you'll learn to really truly hear me. Please just try to observe, and I'll promise to show you the way. The only true way, my way, listen. Often when you make mistakes, I try to give you clear signals like, I lay my ears back and swish my tail, hollow my back, lift my head and neck up high, so I am above the bit. You have little or no control then, it all started to fall apart."

"Mentally and emotionally I have lost it. I cannot take sometimes the level of confusion, for me, it is chaos, and I am afraid and want to run away. Sometimes I'll just shut down and do nothing, trying to give you time to work it out."

"Please when things are going so badly, think about what it is that you are doing. Look in the mirror, often I'll be a reflection of the level of your inability to communicate with me effectively."

"Some days, let's agree that we have done enough, and we will try again on another day."

"I would like to ask you to understand that I am one of The Creator's most forgiving creatures. May I suggest that at times, you'll just be still and listen to the quiet voice within; trust in that, to tell you what really is happening. Listen to the answer, exhale and let's start again."

"Oh! And please always have a plan, and ride that plan, I like that. Lead and I'll follow. Guide me, show me the way, try to be soft and I'll soften too. Be hard, pulling and unforgiving, and then I'll pull as hard as you can – and a lot more."

"Another thing, stay out of my face as much as possible, use your seat, body movement and legs, I'll respond in return. You do not need the bit all that much. Remember, that whatever is in your brain will come down the reins."

"Let's know no fear together, let's gain each other's trust and confidence, because that's what I really need to be able to do – trust you."

"You are going to have to, first and foremost, search for a deep understanding of me, if you want me to understand you. Therefore, I'll help you to do, what you want me to do. Remember, do not overwork me, never run me out of air, or bore me. It's not required and it is counter productive. There is always a tomorrow, I can forgive you, can you find it in your human heart to forgive me, and move on from there?"

"Try to get in touch with my energy – my vibrations. Look into my face and eyes. Try to read my thoughts, feel my feelings. Try to become one, become a horse, because you must understand, that I can never really enter your world, but I'll share a secret with you, you can – no, you must enter mine."

"Up until now you have done much pulling, kicking, poking and prodding me with bits and spurs and sticks. My hope would be that we can agree to leave it where it belongs, in the past. Let's make a covenant to work together from this day forth. I would like to suggest we embrace, and move together as one."

"Come dance with me; but you must lead. Try to make your wishes clear and simple, and I'll do my best to follow your lead. Show me the way, give me clear, simple choices, set me up for success, I like that."

"Repeat things with me a few times, so I'll get it, and then give me the time to process the information. And finally please make sure you know what you are doing, and be consistent in all that you do with me."

Duke was so careful, and he gently stretched out his front legs, and lay back down on his side, groaned then exhaled, blinked and closed his eyes.

The girl looked around, "what was happening?"

In a moment of confusion and near panic she looked at Duke's outstretched body, he groaned again and snorted. The girl saw his rib cage rise and then fall. "Was he alive? Was he breathing?"

"Yes," it seemed he was.

"Then where had the voice come from?" Looking around again there was no one, just her and Duke, her head was starting to clear.

"No," she thought, "that's silly, it could not have possibly been Duke."

The girl was still on her knees in front of Duke's outstretched front legs. She moved to his side to listen to his heart, she placed her ear to his rib cage, it sounded fine. Duke did not move. The girl, still a little baffled by the experience, thought she would lie against Duke's side and rest for a while.

The girl awoke to the cry of a hawk; she noticed the shadow of the bird as it passed over her. Looking to her right she could see the large Regal Hawk sitting in a tree by the arena fence, his dark rust coloured feathers were complimented by his reddish legging.

"When I ride the horse, I am the horse."

And the hawk was gone.

The girl jumped up, as quickly as she could, dazed and a little unsteady on her feet.

The sudden movements did not go unnoticed by Duke, who was now also on his feet, and was looking towards the tree that the hawk had suddenly disappeared from.

The girl had lost all sense of time, she had no idea how long any of this had taken. Duke seemed just fine, as he played with his water bucket, and then wandered over to visit the horse in the next corral.

The girl was still unsure of the source of what she thought she heard, but decided, while it was still fresh in her mind, to write out two copies on the *Manifestation Cards* she kept in her tack box at the barn. One copy she placed in her knapsack, to take home.

The girl gave Duke some hay in his corral and said "Good Boy," and then headed for home.

On the way home she promised herself to review all of her notes before going to sleep, and also to have a plan for her and Duke for the coming days ahead. She had many movements and exercises to practice with Duke, before returning to the Ole' Man.

Chapter 13

"Let's sit over here for a few minutes, I need a break," said the Ole' Man. He picked up a bent and rather twisted stick, on his way over to the coolness of the welcoming shade of the now familiar rock face.

Duke and the girl followed. The girl stood in silence, watching the Ole' Man, she hasn't seen him for a few days, and today he looked differently. She wasn't sure just what it was, the girl, for a few minutes, with soft eyes gazed at the Ole' Man. Around him, she thought she could see what could only be described as a slight glow, a faint light that seemed to surround him.

The Ole' Man moving slowly and slightly bent over, found a spot and with the twisted stick, which was about four feet long, he reached out and drew a small circle in the sand, and then he continued to complete a larger one around it.

The Ole' Man turned slightly to face the girl and spoke, "I would like to express my heartfelt gratitude for the quality time we have spent together, and I would also like to say that I am so proud of the wonderful progress you have made. I would like to congratulate and praise you for having the courage and discipline to have journeyed thus far,"

"But there is more…"

The Ole' Man walked slowly towards a rock, which he was going to use as a seat, and seated himself comfortably. The circle in the sand laid outstretched before him, almost touching his feet.

He raised the stick, and pointing to a rock across from him, said "please come and sit over here, I think you'll find there is room behind it for Duke to stand."

Duke was only too willing to take a nap within the protection of the rock face, and a chance to enjoy the coolness of the shadows of this day.

The girl, who was not sure just what to expect next, sat down and did not say a word, then tried to make herself more comfortable, she also noticed that she felt relaxed and calm.

There seemed to be a strange stillness and slowness surrounding them. Time somehow seemed to standstill, there was an air of tranquility and peace.

The Ole' Man was the one to break the silence.

"After we first met, you made a choice to return, and had the courage to step into the Circle of Knowledge and Truth. Within the realm of that circle, you stood upon holy ground. Maybe not fully realising it's significance at that moment, but you took it upon yourself to invest in becoming aware and responsible for starting the journey of your own spiritual growth, traveling the path to realization of your own full potential, searching to become all that you came here to be – your True Self, Authentic Self."

The girl frowned, and tried to make herself a little more comfortable. She moved her feet slightly, and yet being careful not to break the circle in the sand that almost touched the tip of her riding boots. "I am really not too sure sometimes of all that is happening with me, but I do know now, that much has improved for Duke and I," said the girl.

"Yes, that is so true, but there is so much more, at a deeper level of understanding. I'll try to explain in a while," said the Ole' Man.

"I think you may well have noticed already that at times, many of your friends and others around you appear not to be always fully present – with you. You know, you are talking to them and yet, you know that they are not really listening to you. They may well be paying attention to something else, like all the noise and chatter that is going on in their heads. They do not mean to be that way, you see – they are in a trance."

The girl smiled and said "yes, I have at times noticed, I would be talking to a friend, sharing some of the new things I have learnt, and how things have changed for Duke and me, but you are right, they seemed somehow to be in their own world."

The Ole' Man replied, "Correct. That's exactly the sort of thing I mean, and here are some of the reasons why, ninety percent of how people conduct their actual whole lives are based largely on their habits, their habitual traits, it is like being locked onto an auto pilot."

"Habitually, being reactive displaying the same responses, achieving over and over the same old results. You even see it with people and their horse problems, instead of trying to find a new approach or solution, they do the same old thing, and the horse is guaranteed to respond in the same old way."

"It is like being emotionally stuck in the mud of Life, they are spinning their wheels not progressing very far, and then sometimes briefly getting free, only to find themselves stuck again."

"Even not for one moment, am I trying to judge what is going on in other people lives, they are after all on their own paths, and so be it.

I am just using it as a comparison, and not trying to make it personal. However, let's consider the possible differences while choosing to be conscious, aware, awake and thoughtful, then choosing to take the best possible Right Action."

"Just a minute, I am not sure what all this means, it sounds rather complicated, and just how does it help Duke and I," asked the girl.

"I understand, but bear with me. The good news is that there is always a way out of this stuck state that often so many of us find ourselves in. And so, this is what I would like to try to share with you – becoming unstuck, leading to a personal lasting freedom."

The Ole' Man paused, took a deep breath and continued, "You know, sometimes in our lives, we take a little fall, much like you did off Duke. This comes to people in many ways or messages; often it is a call for an opportunity to wake up. How do we say here – 'to wake up and smell the coffee.' It is a chance to become a little more aware of what is going on in one's life, a chance for us to change, to grow and develop into what could be called – our True Self, Authentic Self."

"I started awhile back to say, that there was so much more, that can take us to a deeper level of understanding. I have the confidence in you, and I believe that the time has come to share with you the fullness of the messages. I am going to ask you to be patient, still your mind of whatever thoughts you have going on, become relaxed and calm, and be fully present in the moment while I share with you these Universal Truths."

"You started by asking for the horse of your dreams and you are well on your way to achieve that dream."

"But, there is still more…"

"Now, I am asking you a far more profound question. Are you ready to work on, or towards *the life* of your dreams?"

The girl answered "I am a little concerned, it still sounds rather complicated, but I am interested and ready to listen to more, please go on."

"Good, I am so glad you have decided to continue on this ever lasting empowering journey of self discovery. Let me try to explain further, how within the Circle of Knowledge and Truth there are, what I call, the Circles of Influence."

"They are all interconnected and yet, interdependent. They constantly influence each other in a wholesome and healthy manner, being Holistic and Synergistic. There is a golden thread of light flowing between them, as they slightly overlap each other in an ever changing state of fluidity. There can be no exact order to them, because it becomes slightly different for each person who accepts them, always relative to that person's present stage of growth."

"Is that clear so far," said the Ole' Man.

Frowning, "I think so," said the girl.

The Ole' Man reached out with the twisted stick and drew another circle in the one laid out before his feet. These are the Circles of Influence. The Ole' Man then wrote two words in the sand, *Awareness* and *Mindfulness*. Looking radiant and happy with himself, as he pointed at the words with the stick, the Ole' Man continued, "Once you become aware, that you have to take control over your mind, that becomes central to the whole process of your personal growth."

"If, in life, we choose not to become aware, there's the risk of a great danger ahead, because then the mind is not called to order, and the mind is then in control, and it is indeed a tricky character."

"If we are not careful and mindful, we can become enslaved within the confines of our own minds, guilty over the years, sometimes without being aware of building walls. We may become prisoners of our own stories, trapped within these boundaries, becoming confused and overwhelmed with the nonsense of our past, sentencing ourselves to a life far less than we came here to fulfill. Therefore, denying ourselves the promise of an enlightened and bright future."

"It may seem strange, but the mind only knows the past stories, events and concepts that we have chosen to nurture and harvest. It does not even know the difference between, what has been termed, 'real' by us, or that which we have simply imagined to be so."

"However, please realise this, we all have been given the authority to make a personal choice to control our own mind, it's called Free Will. The responsibility is to use it wisely; the prize is to be able to change your life. Out of that desire to change, the seeds of greatness are sown."

The Ole' Man looked up at the girl, "do you realise now how important it is to be aware, and to then take control of your mind?"

"I believe I do, because I became aware that I wanted a different relationship with Duke, and you have now helped to make it even clearer for me, that working with Duke has helped; also by always having a plan, which gave me something to refocus on, to give a thought to. Although at times, I would find my thoughts wandering to something else, and then I would try to get back on track. Is that the start of becoming aware," asked the girl.

"Yes, that's wonderful, you are getting the idea," said the Ole' Man.

"Let's go deeper, here is the next part." The Ole' Man bent forward and quickly drew another, slightly overlapping, circle and wrote in the sand, *Thought*.

"Remember I said, that the Circles of Influence are all joined together, *Awareness*, *Mindfulness* and *Thought* are so closely related."

"Yes, I think it's all starting to fit together. Do these changes take a very long time to achieve," asked the girl.

"Great question, we can all choose to change literally in a blink of an eye. It's that simple. All we have to do is to make a conscious choice in the sacredness of this moment, to take control over our minds, by choosing to have a completely new and *empowering thought*."

"To start off with, it should be something small, believable and achievable. That is the first baby step towards change. It helps to lay a new foundation within the mind, which over time establishes changes that may well lead to a healthy belief system."

"Remember, we always have to be mindful, paying attention to what is going on in our minds. We have to try always to choose healthy *Right Thoughts*, by setting up healthy boundaries to only allow into the garden of our minds the seeds, which will produce healthy fruits, maturing into the desired results that we want."

"Our new *Right Thought* must be in line with our intention, and we have to be disciplined enough to remain focused on that. We really have to pay attention to what we want. That process becomes your dominant thought, taking place constantly within the storehouse of your mind."

"What do you think so far," inquired the Ole' Man.

"I think I am getting it," said the girl.

"After the fall and our first talk, I did become aware that I wanted a different relationship with Duke. I changed my mind about getting rid of him, and then it gave me a chance to stop and think about some of the new ideas you gave me. I then thought, why not try to work with Duke, to change the way things had been between us in the past."

"That's wonderful," said the Ole' Man, "at times it's a good idea to take time to sill the mind, sitting quietly, learn to check-out and check-in with the new thought. Remember, the mind can be a tricky character, it will still want to hold onto what it knows best, those old habits that it feels so secure in, especially the ones from the past."

"There will be tests, when they come, try to slow down your response-time to the event, be aware, and pay attention by not being reactive, by not giving way to your old habits. Try to hold dear to your heart your new thought, regroup and move on from there."

"I do hope this is all coming together for you, I would encourage you, as soon as you get back home, to take out some of those *Manifestation Cards* that we have been using, and make some quick simple notes. Write on them some key words like *Awareness, Mindfulness* and *Thought*. What do you think?"

"It is quite a bit of information, but I think, that because of all of our previous discussions and work, we are kind of building on that. If I understand you so far, it really means that within this process, I can branch out to other subjects, is that about right," asked the girl.

"Yes, I think you have a pretty good grasp of it so far. There are just a couple of more points to cover, so let's explore this further together," said the Ole' Man.

"This is another major point; you do have to recognise within yourself the need to change. If you cannot qualify this need, change will not happen, because one ingredient will be missing – your willpower."

"Even more powerful than that, is that you must have a strong desire coupled with your need to change something within yourself, and be so fully committed bringing it to fruition, that it merges with your very soul, and that, that thought travels from your head to your heart. It is then nurtured at the very centre of your essence, at the place that you agree to stand and meet your Creator. That very thought has to become the new born again you."

"How do I know, if I am having healthy good thought," inquired the girl.

Sounding rather excited, the Ole' Man said "Brilliant, outstanding, what a thoughtful question. As a guide for the new thought, check with yourself by asking and testing your response with a couple of simple and yet insightful further thought provoking questions. When you do this, certain feelings and emotions will awaken within you, take a note of them."

"Ask: Is this thought empowering, or disempowering me?"

"Is it hurting or helping me to grow?"

"Is it moving me towards or away from that, which I need to change?"

"You have to bear in mind that each thought, planted in the mind, becomes a cause, and it will always produce an effect, wanted or unwanted."

"Please also keep in mind that there is no such thing as failure, it is just to be recognised as not the result you wanted, consider it as a further opportunity for change and growth."

"A long time ago, a wise man said a successful man's journey can be fraught with one mistake after another, yet he is not deterred and chooses to keep on growing."

"So is it alright to make mistakes," said the girl.

"Oh, very much so," said the Ole' Man. "You try to do the very best you can, to make the right choices, but yes, there will be mistakes, it's inevitable – it is part of the journey. When you realise that this particular result is not working for you, review it and change your choice. Do not waste too much time and energy in blaming yourself, or others. Learn to forgive yourself, be kind to yourself, regroup in the mind and move on."

"In this way, you start to take charge of old habits – negative thought patterns, or inappropriate belief systems that no longer serve your highest potential, whilst on your spiritual journey. You are turning your mind from an unruly child to an effective tool for you."

"Now, I think you can see why it is paramount to be aware, in control of our minds and thoughts, it is the cornerstone, the rock upon which all else will be built and will, when solid, stand the test of time." The Ole' Man looked at her thoughtfully.

The girl looked very attentive and fascinated.

"It is time to move on to the next stepping stone in our journey." The Ole' Man drew another circle and wrote two words within that same circle, indicating that they were closely related *Emotions* and *Feelings*.

"At the same time as we gain control over what goes on in our minds, by developing the purity of our Right Thought, it stands to reason and makes perfect sense that our emotions are going to become more mature, less reactive, calmer and more relaxed. We will become, in time, more emotionally stable."

"From here on in, how you actually feel about something or event will never be the same again. At a deeper level, a spiritual and emotional change takes place, causing your body chemistry to change. You'll feel more alive and have more energy than you have ever had in your life. Now, feeling inspired, your actual physical state will change."

"Duke has already noticed the change in you, being the intuitive creature that he is, and so will other people, the changes will be monumental and life altering."

The Ole' Man laid out one more circle, writing in the sand *Physical State* and *Actions*. "Becoming motivated and being in an empowering physical state, generally feeling better about yourself, your self-esteem increases, you feel more powerful and alive than ever before in your life. You are now inspired and have the confidence to take brave new actions."

"These actions become your deeds and what you do, helps to develop and nurture the new you. You are now well on your way."

The Ole' Man was reaching now forward for the last time, and at his feet within a circle he wrote one more word – *Experience*.

"Your perspective of the world has started to change now. The fledgling new you will think, hear, feel and see differently, because you have chosen, through combining these Circles of Influence, first to take control of your mind – created new thoughts, then by nurturing and living new experiences, you'll have literally laid the cornerstone towards the creation of a new reality."

"This has the power to become for you a brave new world."

"A heaven here on Earth."

"Do not be concerned about Duke in all of this. He knows much of this; he lives in the Truth born of The Creator's Spirit. When we get it right and live in the Truth, it's funny how the horse seems to respond to us so much better. When we live in lies and confusion it leads to chaos."

"The horse, being as sensitive as he is, picks up on this by the thousands of little signals we project to him. The horse does not do well within this kind of environment, and some just fall apart, only to be labelled a problem horse. When the truth is that much of the responsibility for the so called problem can be laid at our feet."

The girl was frowning and moved around a little, Duke moved his weight from one hind leg to the other, and quickly drifted off again. "But I have friends, and I do know trainers at the barn where I board Duke, often, the conversation seems to be that some of the horses are better than others, some have problems and some are just no good. What does all that mean? It's a bit confusing."

"Each horse has to be understood as an individual, and that can be complicated, but I take this fundamental position towards their skills and abilities:"

"The horse can do no wrong, a horse is a horse, is a horse."

"If you want the horse to change, the simple answer is that you must change first."

"Well Duke and I have changed," said the girl.

"That's so true that Duke has changed however, he changed, because you took on the challenge and responsibility to improve some of your horse related knowledge and riding skills. Never forget that the mind is central in influencing control over your physical body, as well as many other aspects of your life, but just think for a moment, and take yourself back to whom and how you felt when you fell off Duke," said the Ole' Man.

"Well, let's see, I was on a runaway horse, I was very scared, hanging on for dear life. I was very tense, when he made that turn I could not hold on anymore with my gripping legs and I fell off. At the time I was frustrated, angry and mad at Duke for being so bad. I really thought and believed that it was his entire fault, he was the problem. Some other people had told me that he was a problem horse, and at that time, I believed that."

"And today, do you now understand how within all these Circles of Influence, you alone can choose and have the power to control the circumstances and events in your life, this has helped change not only Duke, but at a much deeper level – you."

The girl smiled at the Ole' Man, Duke moved back over to his other hind leg. "Yes, I really do believe I understand it more now, I am beginning to realise how it all fits together. It's so amazing; I am really riding the horse of my dreams. The tension and fears have gone, I am far more relaxed. Duke and I do have moments when time seems to stand still, and we enjoy each other in a world of our own, and that has become for me the new experience."

"That's wonderful, I am so happy for you," said the Ole' Man.

"Can you see how all encompassing and yet, at the same time quite beautiful, the Circles of Influence all flow together."

The girl thought for a moment, "I am beginning to realise, as I have said. However, it's still a lot of a new information for me. Is there any way that you could help me to remember the information that is within these circles that are before me."

The Ole' Man smiled, "I think so. It will only take a few more minutes, just hold on lightly to Duke's reins, then step quietly into the centre circle, and when you're ready, sit down."

The girl stepped very carefully into the centre circle. Upon doing so, she immediately noticed, that it felt a little strange, and she found herself sitting down into another world.

The girl now found herself completely surrounded by the Circles of Influence. She could feel the fullness and the completeness of them washing over her. In her heart, she felt a glowing sense of warmth and peace. She was now settled and made herself comfortable on the warm desert sand.

The Ole' Man asked for permission to be her guide, while the girl contemplated these further insights.

The girl, feeling completely safe and secure, gave her approval.

"Now I would like you to close your eyes, still your mind, and focus on your breath. I'll be here, I am going simply to guide you circle by circle."

Upon hearing the expression of each circle, I want you to breath in fully and deeply the very essence of the knowledge and insight of each Circle of Influence. Hold your breath for a few moments, then breath out slowly any negative thoughts, that may have tried to enter your mind."

"Then, with the next expression, slowly breath in again."

"Are you ready to begin," asked the Ole' Man.

The girl nodded and said "Yes."

The Ole' Man said "Good, please close your eyes, and I'll continue."

The Ole' Man softly called out the names of the Circles of Influence, and added an occasional key word, as a further anchor to help the girl establish a total recall.

Awareness	–	Awake
Mindfulness	–	Conscious
Thought	–	Empowering Right Thoughts
Emotions	–	Stability
Feelings	–	Less reactive
Physical State	–	Powerful and Alive
Actions	–	Brave and inspired Right Actions
Experience	–	The Cornerstone of a new reality.

When the Ole' Man had completed the Circles of Influence, he asked the girl to continue focusing quietly on her breath, for a few more minutes, which would allow the insights to become a part of her, to become one with her.

When she felt ready, she was to open her eyes, stand up slowly, and have a little stretch. She could be assured that she would retain all that they had shared.

After a few more minutes had passed, the girl opened her eyes, stood up, stretched and very carefully, stepped out of the Circles of Influence and sat down on the rock alongside the still sleeping Duke.

The girl smiled at the Ole' Man and said, "Thank You so much."

The girl was grateful and recognised that she had now acquired another gift, that would help her on her journey towards not only personal growth, but also the opportunity for further spiritual growth, she smiled to herself, realising that her life, as she had known it, would never be the same again.

Circles of Influence™

Chapter 14

"It seems you are now ready to move on to the deeper meaning, shall we?"

The girl's face lit up as she smiled.

"Pay close attention now," the Ole' Man pointed his stick to the very first circle he had drawn in the centre of the larger one and said, "as you can see now, all the Circles of Influence are slightly over lapping each other. Like the petals of a flower in full bloom."

"I have left the most important until last; much of what we have shared so far has been about choosing personal growth. I do believe all growth is spiritual in its essence, at its very core. This can only mean that, while growth initiates from within us, that there resides a greater and more powerful force than what I'll call myself, the mere flesh and blood of the physical world."

"I, personally, choose to believe that there is something outside of me, and yet at the same time very much a part of me, in spirit. It's *original*. Different people and different cultures have come to recognise it by different names. I have grown to know it personally, and call it – The Creator."

"When we choose to take responsibility for our own spiritual growth, we embark on a journey, we all have our work to do, and we have touched on those subjects known as the Inner Circles of Influence. And while we are doing that, opportunities will present themselves to us by crossing the boundaries of the mere physical world, and having at times the chance to share in brief moments, a glimpse into the realm of the unchanging other world, which surrounds us."

The Ole' Man stretched his hand out while saying "The spiritual world, the realm of The Divine, extends an outstretched hand beckoning us, offering an invitation, so that we may reach out and touch the Universal Consciousness of The Creator."

The girl was starting to feel something stirring deep within.

"Within this spiritual world, there resides the mind of The Creator, out of which everything is created, flows and connected. This is the mind out of which Universal Truth and Unconditional Love radiates throughout Creation."

The Ole' Man was still pointing to the middle circle and continued saying "Within this circle I am going to place four key elements *Faith* and *Trust, Unconditional Love* and *Universal Truth*. These are core spiritual aspects connecting us to The Creator's mind. Hold these close to your heart and soul; cherish these always as eternal gifts."

The Ole' Man looked at the girl, who had been quiet for some time now, "You asked a very wise question awhile ago," said the Ole' Man, "Regarding how to measure what a good healthy thought might be."

"Yes, I did," said the girl. "I think I am getting it, first you have to be absolutely clear on what you want, and you always have to be truthful to yourself. Is that about right?"

"Absolutely, you're right on," said the Ole' Man.

"You can test yourself by asking the questions we went over before, which ultimately leads to the wisdom of Know-Thy-Self. However, at a deeper level of understanding, we need to recognise and believe that The Creator is *Truth*, which has to mean absolute purity of the Universal Mind. That The Creator provides *Universal Unconditional Love*. All this transcends and complements your own thoughts, and moves you closer to understanding and living the principles and values of The Creator. Developing a connection between the physical and the spiritual worlds is really much of the work we are to do, while on our journey."

"Our last two words, within this central circle, are *Faith* and *Trust*," continued the Ole' Man. He paused, looking deeply at the girl, and said "You have been so patient listening to, my sometimes, rambling stories."

"Do you remember when you took the fall," asked the Ole' Man.

"Yes, I do," said the girl. "It seems though, that I have lost track of and all sense of time. I am no longer certain of when it was. I do know you have tried to share so much with me since then."

"Do you remember that throughout this journey together, we have spoken of the horse of your dreams, and also the life of your dreams, and that you had to have the courage to seek it?"

"Sometimes, a leap of faith would be required, sometimes these things are not something you can see, hear, or touch." Stressed the Ole' Man

"There were times that I would ask you, before going on to do things with Duke, to have the faith and trust in him."

The girl nodded "Yes, I do remember. I did not understand at first, but now I realise and believe how important that really was. Having improved my riding skills, and improving my understanding of the rules of how things worked, became a huge help. It did move me to a different level, as I developed my faith and trust in Duke, something else transpired from there on."

"I guess you could call it, a different relationship. One built on a higher level of trust and confidence. Then it became like, at times, that our level of communication with each other changed." The girl mused thoughtfully.

The Ole' Man was smiling, "I realised that you are still young, and yet you have already journeyed far. Remember I told you that you are a Child of the Universe."

"You are now well on your way along the path to becoming your Authentic Self. You are now so close to experiencing something with Duke that is truly wonderful."

"There will come a time when you'll be working with Duke at a higher level of understanding, that it will be as though Duke is no longer there – and neither will you."

"There will be a new creation, a spiritual essence; I have experienced this. I call it *Oneness*, beyond the mere physical realm, beyond the level of our normal senses."

The girl could sense the Ole' Man's excitement as he continued.

"Let me tell you a little story, it will help to explain to you why faith and trust, have to be the cornerstone, the rock upon which, with full confidence, we can build everything that we aspire to, in our riding – and in life."

"As I look back, somehow it seems like it may well have been in another life time, and yet it's still as new and as fresh and as vivid as ever," said the Ole' Man in wonder.

"As I walked through the gate, on my way to the pasture, I spotted a bald eagle above the pine trees, to the south of my ranch. A friendly warm air current helps it to ascend, up and over the ridge, then quickly out of sight. On its way to one of its favourite hunting grounds, the grassy slopes leading down to the Fraser river."

"A little further along, I noticed that the Pussy Willows are still hugging the banks of the creek, and have survived the heavy snow falls of this winter, just passed. They were even brave enough to have green buds busting at the tips of their slender branches, a sure sign of the promise of spring."

"All of a sudden, the unexpected splash of a beaver tail, serves to remind me that I would have to lower a couple of the beaver dams, to the east of me, to help avoid the flooding of the adjoining pasture lands."

"It was an unusually warm spring day, in mid April, for this part of the country."

"At the end of a well worn game trail, I stepped into a large grassy clearing where I came across the foals laying down, having been recently fed by the mares' warm sweet and rich milk, they all seemed quite content. I wandered amongst the spring crop, the odd ear twitched, the occasional head moved slightly, with an eye that was partly opened, and then settled back down into the lush Timothy and Brome grass."

"Satisfied that all was well, I went over to sit on a log by the edge of the creek. Settled, I closed my eyes, enjoying one of those rare still moments."

"Let's just say, that recently there had been some events in my life that had really brought me to my knees. Finding myself at the cross roads of my understanding of how life was supposed to work and therefore, my faith in general had been shaken to its core."

The Ole' Man's expression became intense as he described "A soft warm breeze seemed to wash over me. Then it came to me, as in a vision, I saw a large old fashion loom, out of which flowed the very fabric of life."

"It's his design – The Creator's – and he's the master weaver."

"I was shown that, we are but a mere thread, always in his presence, as a part of the pattern. It seems we never go away."

"I saw written:

An oath was given – a promise made.

Then as The Creator continues to weave the ever-evolving tapestry;

He lays out reality before us."

"That this is the True Source of all creativity, purity of thought and mind, including Unconditional Love – and Absolute Divine Truth."

"I was also shown that, in full confidence, I could have the faith and trust in all these things being revealed to me."

"Within each and every thread, there is entwined our passion, and our very purpose in life."

"Whilst, all these threads are intertwined and interrelated, mingling up and over and around each other, there are no two threads alike."

"They have all been granted different gifts by The Creator, so that all will have the opportunity to fulfill their individual mission, while exercising their own Free Will."

"All is laid out within this design."

"I was also shown, that above and beyond this richly woven tapestry, is the unseen spiritual world."

"Suddenly, I was awake, feeling refreshed, fully aware, and in full knowledge that I could trust in and have the faith in these things, as they were revealed to me."

"Knowing I could have full confidence in all things hoped for, although unseen and a mystery to me. All of these things are grounded in Absolute Truth, because The Creator cannot lie; and his ways are unchanging."

"I finally understood that I was only to try my best to work within his guidelines – and I would be blessed."

"Faith is being humble enough to believe, that I do not have all the answers, and there is something beyond me that I can trust in impeccably."

"So there you have it. You can choose to be a believer or non-believer."

"If you choose to be a believer, and live by faith, it opens up the possibilities to co-create. Let me say that, those who seem more creative, in whatever they do, are so, because they are participating at a higher level of harmony and unity, connected at a deeper level of relationship with The Creator's Spirit."

"They accomplish this by being fully awake, with a heightened sense of awareness, and a deeper understanding of an unshakeable faith, in that which cannot be seen, or fully comprehended – the mystery of life."

"Yet, they continue to live in full confidence, and in child like awe, that all is taken care of."

"I think we need to just accept that while we live in this physical world, there is beyond the veil, that unseen other world, the world of The Divine Realm."

"This is simply beyond our comprehension."

"Beyond the frailty of our humanness."

"Beyond the simplicity of our verbal expression, to even attempt to describe the Realm of The Divine."

"It's like, we find ourselves, standing at the edge of our Universe, blinking, searching for answers, which only begs more questions."

The Ole' Man took a brief pause and looked at the girl intently saying:

"Throughout the ages, messengers have travelled through the veil to share with those that had the eyes to see, and the ears to hear, some of the many secrets of how to live the most rich, rewarding and successful life, as could be humanly possible."

"Sadly, often, they have been ignored."

The Ole' Man went on further to explain that while in this world, that we are all called to be participators, and not spectators. "Remember that we've touched on this before that we must first take control of our minds – created new thoughts, then by nurturing and living new experiences, we'll have literally laid the cornerstone towards the creation of a new reality."

"While there is nothing fundamentally wrong with questioning, we should find a place in which we grow strong in faith, to seek to be at peace, realising that we will never have all the answers."

"Man will never be able to define, qualify, and quantify everything."

"Why? You may well ask, it's simple, because The Creator is always creating. He will always lead the way, opening the door, being The Light, illuminating the path – The Way."

"We can choose to follow in faith, as willing partners. No doubt we may stumble and fall, only to rise again, press on, go forward, one step at a time, but it will be forever a never-ending empowering journey of self-discovery."

"As the Child of the Universe, I have wanted to share so much with you, but maybe all of this is too much for you, all at once."

"Again, I may gently remind you, that it's always up to you. It is your personal responsibility to choose wisely."

"Remember, within all I have laid before you, you always have the option of Free Will – nothing is being forced upon you."

"The good news is that it will always be there for you in the completeness and fullness of time, whenever you feel ready to take that leap of faith."

"Much of this last part of the Circles of Influence, cannot be worked out by intellect alone. The answer to the riddle of faith cannot be found in the head. Search for it within your soul and ask the Spirit that dwells in your heart, therein lies the answer."

"Well, all this sounds rather grand, and by now I am sure you are wondering whether the Circles of Influence will work for you if you choose to leave out all this other stuff. My answer is a resounding Yes, absolutely, and they will serve you very well indeed."

"However, may I just mention to you, in my humble opinion, that when you choose to combine *all* the elements of the Circles of Influence, as a believer, there is the opportunity to live a life at the highest possible level of awareness, consciousness, and a deeper level of understanding."

"Being fully alive, fully awake in the here and now – in this present moment."

"I understand, this is a lot to share with you, but please bear with me, so I can finish the last little bit on the subject of Trust." Said the Ole' Man noticing the girl looking a little concerned.

The girl was looking and feeling, by now understandably, a little overwhelmed. "I thank you for sharing so much with me. This does seem like a lot of stuff, and of course, it is all new to me, but please go on, as it is getting a little bit late."

"I'll be as brief as possible," said the Ole' Man.

"For me, Trust is built upon the cornerstone, the rock of the Truth born of The Creator's Spirit."

"It's having faith in that Truth, that becomes my anchor. Helping to hold me steady and steadfast, when being battered by the waves of uncertainty, which are all too often whipped up by the winds of this world's ever changing truth."

"Often throughout my life, I have suffered, had doubts and fears, stumbled and strayed from the Light. However, after many years of trying and searching different ways and paths, I can assure you, with full confidence, that the more I am in alignment with the fullness of all the elements of the Circles of Influence – the more I am blessed."

"I know in my heart, that I can live in faith and trust, and the truthfulness of the Circles of Influence, as laid here at your feet."

"Try to remember this, as we try our best to live with the purity of Mindfulness combine with the Right Actions, why it seems to me – miracles happen."

"In a greater sense, it means that we become so much more connected to the realm of The Divine. Then we recognise, that each and every moment is a miracle, as life unfolds around us."

"This is only because we have chosen to live in Faith, connecting us in a strange and yet, beautiful and mystical way, to The Creator's Spirit. With that, we are blessed with abundance beyond our imagination."

"In part, this approach is about us, as human beings, desiring to make changes in our spiritual growth and about becoming the best we can possibly be, through the medium of trying to truly understand one of God's most noble creatures, our friend the horse. In choosing to do so, we embark on a journey to understand ourselves more fully."

Circles of Influence™

Chapter 15

The next few days, following the girl's last meeting with the Ole' Man, became a time of mixed dreams, thoughts and contemplations.

The girl found time to write, as much as she could recall on her *Manifestation Cards*, and would review them before riding, and before going to sleep.

The girl made a promise to herself, to continue this for the next thirty days, then record her results.

Duke and the girl enjoyed some nice trail rides, and she continued her riding in the large outdoor arena. They were doing very well, the riding and the relationship had improved greatly.

While out riding in the desert, the girl had tried to ride some large circles. Duke, would at times, fuss with his head, and do some strange things with his hind-end. While returning to the barn, the girl stroked Duke's neck, "Good Boy Duke," she said, "I think it's about time we returned to see if the

Ole' Man could offer some help to improve our circles."

The next day, Duke and the girl set off along the familiar trail to seek some further help from the Ole' Man.

It had been about a week since their last meeting. The Ole' Man seemed happy to see them riding towards him, as he sat relaxing in the shade.

The girl rode up to him, "I'm so glad to see you. Duke and I've been doing a lot since our last meeting. The fact is, so much has improved, and before I forget, I want to thank you for all you've shared with me, the last time we were together."

The girl laughed, "I've made lots of notes."

"Why, that's great," said the Ole' Man, as he stood up and reached to stroke Duke's neck.

Duke, very gently, turned his head and lightly touched the Ole' Man's arm.

"Come and sit for a few minutes, and tell me how things have been going for the two of you. What have you done and written," said the Ole' Man.

They sat for a while, and the girl recounted how she had been doing and asked for clarification on a few points.

The Ole' Man was happy to do so, and it gave him a further opportunity to share more secrets and insights with the girl.

"Well," said the Ole' Man after a while, "let's spend some time on helping you improve your understanding of riding a nice circle."

The Ole' Man put his Side Reins on Duke, and lunged him within the Circle of Knowledge and Truth. Happy that Duke was going well and nicely warmed up, the Ole' Man asked the girl, "Do you know what train tracks are like?"

"Yes, I do," said the girl, "why? What does that have to do with riding a circle?"

The Ole' Man went on to explain, "I'm going to use the track, as a concept, forming a large circle."

"I want you to imagine riding that circle, and Duke's inside feet will be on the inside rail, and of course, his outside feet will follow the contour of the outside rail."

"Do you see that small bush over there? That's going to give you a focal point, as the centre of your circle, is that clear?"

"Yes," said the girl, "I think so."

"Well, up you get onto Duke, and let's head over there." The Ole' Man asked the girl to just ride around the small bush, about thirty feet away from it, to get an idea of the size of the circle, she would be working on.

The Ole' Man said "this will go really easily, because of all the foundational work you have already done. Duke will move his head and neck softly, wherever you wish it to be, also his hip and rib cage will move, responding to various degrees of pressure, and or support from your legs."

"All we have to do now, is give Duke the required directions for him to understand, that he is to stay on the circle. Are you ready," asked the Ole' Man.

"Yes," said the girl.

"Fine, just let Duke Walk On, I am going to start with your hands. You are going to the left, so in this case your inside hand is going to be your left hand. It has a very simple job to do, all it has to do is ask Duke to bend his head and neck, so you can just see his eye."

"Go ahead and ask for that, and as you do just maintain contact with your outside rein – right rein, to control and maintain the degree of bend."

"This outside rein is the most important. It also controls the speed and the impulsion. Later on, when Duke gets really good at this, you'll be able to actually give the inside rein away, and he will maintain the curve, which is being defined by the outside rein."

"Now, let's add your legs, your inside left leg, is placed at the girth. This is what the horse bends around. By applying pressure with this leg, through the horse to your outside rein, helps to further define the curve of the circle."

Duke was going quite well, but was moving the hind-end off the circle, to the right. The girl realised this, and asked the Ole' Man, "but, Duke is going crooked, what do I do now?"

"That's where your other leg comes in, the outside leg, your right, move it to wherever it is needed in order to move that body part over. In this case, move it behind the girth, four to six inches, and apply pressure to move Duke's hip back onto the curve of the track, while you continue to maintain your other aids in place," explained the Ole' Man.

The girl moved her right leg, and Duke responded by moving over.

"Now move your leg back to its neutral position, at the girth, supportive and passive, yet ready to respond, as required."

"Good," said the Ole' Man, "that's going very well. Just let me give you a little bit more information, with regards to your upper body, just sit up straight, naturally, without tension or stiffness. At times, if needed, as a driving aid – just practice bracing your lower back, Duke will feel that through your seat and it will encourage him to move forward."

"Remember to soften your hands, which will help to develop self carriage, that means Duke will not come to rely on you holding his front-end up, and of course, seek to praise him as much as possible, whenever you can."

The Ole' Man was smiling, "that's a very good start. At home, you can place some buckets, as markers, to define the outside track, also place one in the centre. They can become reference points for you, and help you maintain a sense of where you are."

"While you are riding, try to visualise and feel the horse, as a coil of fluid energy, that there are waves of energy that flow with each stride, travelling through the horse, and that you catch the energy in your hands. You soften and release, it flows down through Duke's front legs into the ground, and back up through the hind legs."

"This is the wellspring of equestrian activity, and it is the life force to a higher level of riding, which, if pursued, will then become an art form."

"What do you think so far," said the Ole' Man.

"I feel it is going very well, Duke is being so kind. Again, I think, at times, I've been just confusing him, because he did these circles very well, I thought. It's all coming together, I'll continue with this at home, and I even think I'll practice around some trees on my trail rides."

"That sounds great, just keep practicing perfect-practice at the walk, have patience, when you think Duke is ready then go on to trot. When you're confident that it's solid at the trot, then, and only then, proceed to a slow canter. If at the canter you find that it's not going well, then you can always continue practicing at the walk and trot."

"Do remember, often the slow way is the fast way, while training horses. Always try your best to establish a level of excellence, while practicing a particular movement at a certain gait, before increasing the degree of difficulty."

"If you still have some time, would you be interested in a couple of more exercises, that would help you develop more suppleness and control of Duke's body," asked the Ole' Man.

"That would be wonderful," said the girl. "What sort of exercises are they? Are they very difficult to do?"

"No," said the Ole' Man, "especially given all the training and conditioning that Duke has now. We will be just really building on that. I am sure Duke will come through for you with flying colours, given all the skills he now has."

"Sounds fine," said the girl. "What do I have to do, I am ready to move on."

"Well," said the Ole' Man, "we're first of all going to go ahead and refine the leg-yielding, so that instead of Duke travelling at a slight angle, when you've been practicing it along your fence line, Duke will now travel sideways at ninety degrees to the fence line."

"It will be easier for Duke to start with, if his head is pointing slightly in the direction of travel, later on, as he improves, his head and neck will be in line with his body."

"Is that fairly clear," inquired the Ole' Man.

"I've never done that before, but it sounds alright. Duke does leg-yielding both ways, I think quite well," said the girl.

"Excellent," said the Ole' Man, "ride over to the rock face that we used before to practice the leg-yielding, and go to the right. Go through, two or three times, just to loosen Duke up."

When the girl came around again, the Ole' Man said, "after a couple of strides, reach back a little further with your left leg, to move Duke's hind-end over a little more to the right, asking him to be at a right angle to the rock face. Try to maintain a balanced feel in your hands to support his head and neck."

"The next time you'll come around, I'll help by walking in line with your girth."

Duke and the girl tried a couple of more times with the Ole' Man helping just a little. It all went very well.

"There, I told you it would be easy for you and Duke, I am very pleased with both of you." The Ole' Man went on further to explain why it is so important to be able to supple and control the individual parts of the horse's body.

The Ole' Man then spent a few more minutes teaching Duke and the girl how to progress from the side-pass to a turn on the forehand, and then a turn on the haunches.

"It's all just a matter of refinement, once the foundational training is solid." The Ole' Man stroked Duke's neck, "There's a smart boy, and you young lady, you did very well indeed."

"What do you think so far? Do you feel you are getting an understanding of how these movements help you in your riding?"

"Oh yes," said the girl, "it feels great to have Duke respond to the requests of my leg. This really gives me even more to build on, I'll continue to try these movements at home."

"Good, because I now would like to take the opportunity to show you the exercise that combines these movements, I call it riding the circle-square. I am sure you'll enjoy it and it will be of great benefit for both of you. Would you like to try it?"

"Yes, of course, I would, the circle-square you said, how does that work?"

"Let's go back to the Circle of Knowledge and Truth." On the way over, the Ole' Man picked up four small sticks, he then placed them on the edge of the circle. The four points then defined a square within the circle, which was about sixty feet across.

The Ole' Man continued to explain, "as you can see, we now have a square within our circle. Now, because Duke know's how to do a rein-back, leg-yielding, side-pass, turn on the forehand and haunches, we are now going to combine them, along the lines of this square."

"Oh, I think I am beginning to get it. Let's get started," said the girl.

The Ole' Man went and stood in front of one of the sticks, "ride over here and face me," said the Ole' Man.

Duke and the girl rode up to the Ole' Man, and did a nice halt. Duke's head almost touched the Ole' Man's chest. Duke's hind legs were well placed and square under him. Duke was on the bit, awaiting further instructions, and ready to move off anywhere.

The Ole' Man covered Duke's eyes with his hands for a few moments, he then stepped to Duke's side and laid his hands on Duke withers.

The girl inquired, "what are you doing?"

"I'm blessing and thanking him, and telling him that I've faith in him to do what I would like him to do, and that I trust him to do all you ask of him. I'm going to get you started, and after that you're on your own to do whatever you wish," said the Ole' Man.

"Before you start, just sit for a few minutes, still your mind and relax. Concentrate on your breath, try not to think too much. Seek to go beyond thought, become aware. Understanding is in the doing. Just softly respond to whatever happens, moment by moment. Trust in your body's wisdom."

"Remember the Circles of Influence, ride in Faith and Trust, feel the ride, and Duke will respond accordingly."

"Are you ready," asked the Ole' Man.

Looking very calm and relaxed, the girl responded, "yes, I am."

"Then begin with rein-back to the stick directly behind you – then continue from there, to whatever movements you feel like doing, until you wish to finish."

The Ole' Man went and sat in the shade, and smiled as he watched the girl and Duke ride the square within the Circle of Knowledge and Truth.

The girl and Duke went ahead and did leg-yielding, side-pass to a corner, a turn on the forehand, another smooth rein-back to the next stick, around and around they went, in a world of their own.

After a few more minutes, the girl brought Duke to a perfect halt right by the stick, at which she had started. She put the reins in her left hand, leaned forward and stroked Duke's neck. "Good Boy, Duke."

On a loose rein, she rode over to join the Ole' Man in the shade of the rock face. The Ole' Man stood up reaching Duke, he stroked Duke's neck and withers.

"Well, well, Duke, you're truly amazing. What a fine performance." The Ole' Man looking at the girl said "and you, young lady, I'm so proud of you. You have truly ascended to a new level of understanding."

"Let's sit for a few minutes, the ride looked wonderful, how did it feel to you?"

Duke found a place in the shade, and the Ole' Man and the girl made themselves comfortable.

The girl, elated, said "It was a truly wonderful *experience*. One, I am sure, I'll never forget. Thank you so much for helping to make it all become possible for Duke and I."

"Thank you," said the Ole' Man. "Now, can you share with me, what it was like?"

"Well, let's see," said the girl, "I am sure that this might sound a bit strange, it was as though Duke and I became one. It was so amazing, it felt effortless, as we flowed from one movement to another."

"To start with, I did have a thought of what to do, but from there on, it became just a matter of doing. In fact, I felt I was achieving so much more by doing less. At times, it seemed instant, I would just have a thought, and even before the thought was completed, Duke was doing it. It was more intuitive, Duke responded to my every wish. At times, just looking in a certain direction, and he would already be going that way. I lost all sense of time, because I felt we were just in this space, of the here and now."

"Somehow it seemed, like we were in another world. With regards to using my hands and legs, I'm not sure what to say. I don't think I was conscious of physically doing much at all. All I now know, you told me once that there would come a time, at a higher level of consciousness, that Duke would not be there, and neither would I, but a new state of Oneness."

"You had described that it would be beyond our normal physical senses, well, I believe in that case – this is what I have just had the privilege to experience," concluded the girl.

"I'm so happy for you and, of course, Duke. This is an example of the fullness and completeness of the Circles of Influence being expressed in this new experience for you. This indeed is something you can cherish. You've now laid the cornerstone, the rock, upon which you can develop new and exciting riding experiences."

"Not only that, and maybe far more importantly, I'm sure you're beginning to realise that you do have the power and the authority to build the life of your dreams."

"My hope would be, that you'll take this information and weave it into the very fabric of your life."

The Ole' Man was slightly bent over, sitting on the rock, and looking a little tired.

They sat in silence for a few moments, as the sun was descending, casting its evening shadows across the Circles of Influence stretched out before them, in the desert sand.

The Ole' Man broke the silence. "Today, this new experience became a stepping stone into the world of your new reality."

"*Experience* was, if you remember, the last of our Circles of Influence."

"You've now transcended being only confined to the physical world. Now you are free. Be like the Hawk of the Desert, with arms outstretched, take flight – soar."

It was getting a little late, the girl said "I'll continue to practice what you have shared with me, and I'll make some notes, as soon as I get back to the barn. Thanks again."

The Ole' Man continued to sit in the shade, smiled and was content, as he watched them ride away.

Chapter 16

A few days later, the girl was at the local tack store. She knew the lady who was behind the counter, in fact, the lady owned the store, and sometimes taught lessons in the area. The store owner asked the girl the usual questions of how is your horse doing.

The girl said "He was doing just fine," and that she was getting some help. Things started to improve for her and Duke; both were much calmer, relaxed and confident in each other than they had ever been. He was coming along nicely getting more responsive day by day.

While serving someone else, the owner casually asked, "Who?"

"I am not sure of his name," said the girl, "an Ole' Man. I've met him at times on my rides in the desert."

The girl was picking up one of the magazines on the sales counter, "Will that be all?" The store owner said to the lady buying a large bag of dog's food, and then via the intercom gave instructions to the boy in the warehouse to load the lady's car.

The magazine fell open in the girl's hands; she could not believe her eyes. There was the Ole' Man! Even though the photo was taken from behind, as he looked up at a beautiful young lady on a magnificent warm blood dressage horse, with hundreds of people watching seated in the stands. There was no mistaking it, it was the Ole' Man from the desert.

The owner, could not help but notice that some colour had drained from the girl's sun tanned face. Almost shaking, fixed on the photograph in the magazine, "anything wrong dear?"

"That's him!"

"What do you mean?"

"That's him," said the girl, "the Ole' Man in the desert, the one who has been helping Duke and I."

Even with the magazine up side down in the girl's hands, the store owner recognised a world renowned teacher, who was known to travel in many parts of the world, but to the best of her knowledge, he had never been to this part of this country. "Oh! I don't think so dear," said the store owner.

"Yes, it is, Yes it is!" Said the girl, "I have spent much of this spring break with him and Duke, out in the desert. "I think he really tried to help me a lot."

The article was a tribute to the man's lifetime of work helping horses and people around the world.

She put the magazine down on the counter and in complete disbelief left the store.

The store owner served couple of more people and almost forgot about the girl and the magazine, it was now quiet for a few minutes, and she picked up the magazine and found the photograph the girl had been looking at. Yes, she was right, she knew who he was.

The girl was planning to go riding in the next couple of days, as usual, nothing formal had been arranged. The Ole' Man often just said, "Well, I think that's enough for Duke for today, and I can still be available, if you wish," and they would say Goodbye and part.

The very next day, the girl, could not wait to ride out into the desert once more, and she was going to confront the Ole' Man and find out just who he was, and tell him about the magazine story. When she reached the top of the familiar sand dune, she looked into the distance expecting to see the Ole' Man waiting in the circle, or sitting on the rocks nearby where she had sat and asked him so many questions.

Sometimes, she had just been gently led to find her own answers from within, which at times, the Ole' Man reassured her, they were there all the time, just waiting for an opportunity to find a way out.

Only she could not see him, Duke whinnied, she thought maybe he was late, but he had always been there for her before.

When she reached the circle, she dismounted, led Duke to the centre of the circle, there she found the Ole' Man's stick in the sand with the small soft rope coiled laid to one side, and a small rolled piece of paper.

Duke sniffed the rope, lifted up his head high looking to the horizon and whinnied again, and then he lowered his head snorted and pawed at the sand near the rope.

The girl, holding Duke's reins, sat down in the centre of the Circle of Knowledge and Truth, quietly waiting for the Ole' Man to come. Suddenly, she heard the cry of a Regal Hawk far above her in the deep blue desert skies, and a soft voice whispering:

"Continue to feel and listen to your horse;"

"Continue to feel and listen to your heart;"

"Continue to feel and listen to your soul;"

"Continue to control your mind and thought;"

"Find times to be still and listen to the quiet voice within;"

"Seek to have peace of mind;"

"Seek to have peace in body;"

"Seek to have peace in spirit;"

"Continue to seek your Creator;"

"Continue to live in Truth and Unconditional Love;"

The girl felt confused and somewhat disappointed, gathered up the Ole' Man's stick, rope and the rolled piece of paper and put them in her pocket, and mounted Duke.

Back the next day at the tack store, the girl picked up the magazine, looked at the article briefly while standing in the corner of the store, recognising some of the information she had heard from the Ole' Man in the desert. At the end of the article, was a fond farewell note from the editor to the man who had died a couple of months ago in England, just after having finished a clinic.

The girl made up her mind to purchase the magazine, and hurried back to the barn. There, she sat on her tack box, holding her *Manifestation Cards*, she settled to read the article in depth.

The journalist prompted the Ole' Man with some regular general questions, which the Ole' Man answered in a more profound way:

"All I know is, when I work with horses, I feel blessed, gifted with endless energy and completely focused. Insights and creative ideas flood into my very being. I have experiences at a deeper level of understanding, because I feel I am in another world. While I realise this may sound a little crazy to some people, it's like I am vibrating at a different level, fully alive and totally aware, yet in a healthy state of being, completely in the moment."

"At this higher level of consciousness, there is a flow of energy between the horse I am working with and myself. Becoming completely engrossed in the whole horse, I try my best to completely and fully understand everything the horse is communicating to me, physically, emotionally, and I'll even venture to say spiritually."

"At this level, I have the rare opportunity to become one with the horse, to enter into the realm of the horse's world. To have an opportunity to both see and feel, and experience the world through his eyes, through his heightened senses."

"This is far removed from the mere physical realm of kicking and pulling of the reins."

"At this transcended level I am trying to describe, a mere suggestion of thought will cause the horse to complete a movement, whether you are on the ground working your horse, or in the saddle. Once you have experienced this level of communication, once you have shared this emotional bond with the horse, I doubt very much that anyone would return to the old ways of treating the horse, as only a mere physical creature."

"Once you have lifted the lid of this box, and looked inside expecting to find a fully authentic physical, emotional and spiritual being, with a full range of senses, including a wide range of personalities and character traits, much like our own – there is no going back."

"Now, we have the responsibility and the opportunity to respect all that it means. We find ourselves in a new world, from which we can choose to build a very different relationship."

"Let's be perfectly clear here, I am not for one moment trying to humanize the horse. I am fully aware of the size of the horse's brain, but it is far more than that."

"The horse has been observing us humans, for at least as long as we have been observing them. I have a reason to believe that they – the horse, may well have been the more intuitive observer. Therefore, horses may well have as much to teach us, as we have to share with them."

The Ole' Man was coming now to a more practical issue and continued by saying:

"In this fast paced 21st century of ours, instant-replay physical world, video games and, *I want it now!* mentality, where many of us find ourselves highly stressed, and maybe are addicted to our past challenges, fears and concerns, the possibility of riding and enjoying our horses can go a long way towards helping us become more grounded or centered, relative to a quality way of life for ourselves, or our loved ones."

"The following, I have found, helps me and my horses, to try and be in the right place:"

"I would like to share with you that deep inside all of us, there is a genius trying to get out. We have all the qualifications and skills required to do and be all that we want to be. It is just that sometimes, because of many reasons, these things have become suppressed."

"For me, there is a higher power – The Creator, available to us all to help provide all the skills and resources we need. We just need to get in touch with it, you may have heard the ancient saying "Ask, and you shall receive.""

"This helps raise our awareness of many things, it empowers us and allows us to operate at a higher conscious level of understanding, which means becoming more aware of the spiritual aspects of all that is Life, as well as improving all that is physical for us. Joining the two worlds will mean a more balanced approach to riding and life in general, and in all that, we endeavour to do or be."

"I would like to encourage the readers to try the following before they ride or train their horse:"

"Still the mind, stop the thoughts from racing;

Breathe fully and deeply;

Exhale the frustrations and cares of the day;

Say a little prayer;

Meditate on your riding plan for the day;

Visualise your ride at a high level of excellence;

Become calm – connected to your horse;

Get in touch with nature;

Breathe in all the beauty that surrounds you, see, smell and feel it;

Become quiet – still, yet confident;

Open all your senses to all that is around you;

Lay your hands on your horse;

Praise him;

Thank him;

Join with him and ride him."

"Your horse, being the intuitive creature that he is, will notice a big difference in your emotional and physical state. You'll feel a big difference in your horse during this ride."

The girl read again the fond farewell note from the editor to the man who had died a couple of months ago in England, just after having finished a clinic, and was filled with both sorrow and wonder. How could it be that he appeared to her in the desert?

The girl got up and went to look for Duke. She needed his closeness and friendship, she suddenly felt quite lonely. Duke was grazing in his corral; he immediately picked his head up and focused on her, he approached her even before she called him.

Once they met in the middle of the corral, Duke, very gently rested his head on the girl's shoulder. He had never done this before, and it caught the girl completely by surprise, she could not move, but was able to reach up with her arms and place them around Duke's neck.

"Duke you silly boy, what are you doing?"

When all of a sudden the girl heard quite clearly, a soft smooth voice say:

"I want to share more with you. I feel that you have grown enough to hear this message."

"My ancestors have told stories from generation to generation, of the close relationship we have had with humans. That our psyches and souls have become entwined, as they became woven into the very fabric of history, going back as far as any one can remember, before the dawn of time."

"We did not choose to be a part of much that has happened. Many did not treat us well, at times we have been considered disposable. We have been with you during your wars, journeys and adventures, failures and triumphs, shared in your joys and pain."

"Now we long for a new relationship, we believe we have earned it. It is time for a change in our relationship, if you were only receptive, you could learn so much about yourselves, by listening to us. You should become more aware, understand and accept this."

"We understand so much about you as humans, because of our common bonds. The fact is, that our insights come from thousands of years of collective consciousness, stored at a spiritual level passed on from soul to soul."

"This is why we understand you so well, you cannot deceive us, cannot fool us; we have lived with you for so long."

"While it is true that we live in the moment, we have developed a heightened sense of intuitiveness. This is why we respond to and understand your emotions, feelings, and read your physical states so easily."

"We try to tell you and give you messages. Some have started really to listen. We call them the healthy ones. Those that are centred, grounded mentally, and are emotionally stable."

"For us they are a joy to be around, to dance with and perform our best for. We can feel safe and be at peace with them."

"You are so fortunate to have met the Ole' Man, he is among them, we call them – Kindred Spirits."

"Unfortunately, there are still others, who are anxious, have fears and concerns with unresolved past issues therefore, generally unstable. Of course, we sense these things, we become afraid and concerned. It puts us in a state of high alert. We want to take flight, and to go into self preservation mode. Combined, it heightens our level of sensitivity. Then these kinds of humans tend to label us spooky, unbroken or worse yet, a problem horse that needs retraining."

"If more humans would just listen more, try to observe and seek to understand, and be in harmony with the laws of nature, real growth and healing would take place. Changes would also take place at a spiritual level."

"In this century, this is our hope for the future. That many more humans will get in touch with spiritual growth, and that we can help them find the road to a healing experience. If they would just open their hearts, minds and souls, and accept us, as a reflection of what's going on within them."

"You see, sometimes when they think they are having a problem with us, they are the problem. There are no problem horses, just some people projecting their problems onto their horse."

"There's an old saying my mother used to tell me Show me your horse, and I'll tell you who you are."

"Well, I think that's more than enough for the time being, but remember to be receptive and aware, and messages and insights will flow to you."

Duke slowly and very gently lifted his head from its resting place on the girl's shoulder. They looked deep into each other's eyes and time had ceased to exist. It would be Duke, who moved first taking a couple of steps back, he then stopped, laid down and had a good roll, got up and shook himself, dust flew everywhere, he then walked off to eat a little hay.

The girl somewhat shaken, looked around in complete disbelief, no one was around. She did feel a little tired and had lost complete track of time, but was confused and unsure of what had just taken place.

Could it really be that the voice she had heard was that of Duke, at that very moment Duke lifted his head from eating his hay and turned to look at the girl, Duke's eyes locked onto the girl's.

"Yes it is I, be not afraid."

Duke shook his head slowly from side to side, lowered his gaze and went back to the task of finishing his snack.

This girl went home, and decided to tell no one of what had occurred.

Suddenly, the girl remembered the rolled paper that was in her pocket, and hurried to take it out. She found that it was a note that the Ole' Man had left her, and it said:

"Congratulations! You have had the courage to embark on an empowering journey, acquiring new skills and knowledge. This has created the possibility for you to make Right choices; the responsibility for that action is yours alone."

"This is most important; I want you to recognise that you now have the Power to have the horse, life or world that you would like to create."

"To start off with, you applied your thoughts to manifesting the horse of your dreams, now you can apply this process to anything you desire in life, so do remember, that which becomes your dominant thought, becomes even more powerful when it is in alignment with your true purpose or passion in life."

"I am not, for one moment, wanting to mislead you, not everything will be easy, and it's not just a matter of wishing for something to happen. Oh no, it will require hard work, and the Right actions to be taken by you. There may be some delays, and not everything that you want will show up within your timeframe, but you'll find, as you remain dedicated and disciplined in your Right thoughts, that it's surprising how opportunities will present themselves – doors will open before you, resources and people will show up."

"Still you'll always be required to take the responsibility to make choices, try always to choose wisely. You may make mistakes, there will be little warning signs along the way that say – slow down, lessons to be learned."

"Learn to listen to the still quiet voice from within."

"First and foremost, be patient and kind to yourself, learn as quickly as you can, that which you need to learn. Try to find it in your heart to forgive yourself, and others when that should be the case, and then regroup and move on."

"Leaving the past where it belongs – in the past, remember you only have, and can live in this moment, do not therefore taint it with the past, and do not confuse it with the future, for it will take care of itself, by you paying attention to the fullness and quality of the moment at hand."

"And so with the sunset of this day, we can be assured of the promise of the dawn of the morrow."

"As with all endings, there can only be the promise of new beginnings."

The girl never saw the Ole' Man again.

The End

About the Author

Robert McLardie was born in Sherwood Forest, with a horse at the bottom of the garden path, Nottinghamshire England.

Robert has been able to trace his family name with the history of being messengers, being known as the King's speakers or Heralds throughout the Isles of Scotland.

Today, Robert believes he is just delivering the message, in part he is being used to share with you the insight that he has been given regarding understanding horses, people, relationships and spiritual growth.

Robert has had the experience of ranching in BC Canada, even using a team of horses and a bob-sleigh to haul hay in the winter.

For over 35 years Robert has been a breeder and trainer of Arabs, Quarter horses, and Warm Blood Thorough bred crosses.

During Robert's working life time he has been also involved in the construction industry, and has worked on a large variety of building projects including the designing of Equestrian centres, Barns, Riding Arenas and Round-Pens.

Robert has ridden horses on Cariboo trails in Grizzly bear country, along the Alpine meadows of the Artic Water Shed in Northern BC Canada.

He has trained wild horses from the High Country of Montana, USA.

Robert once trained a ten year old wild horse to respond to an eight year old autistic boy, who eventually could communicate and work with the horse in a round-pen and ride him.

To winning a Super Horse competition, Robert has shown horses at CEF, AQHA and IAHA shows, covering a full range of classes including halter, English, Western, Eventing and Driving.

Well traveled Robert, to further his education, has visited many fine Equestrian centres throughout England, Canada and the USA.

While on one of his visits to England, Robert was invited to the Nottingham Mounted Police Division training school, and had the opportunity to ride Saxony, a 16.2H police horse.

It would seem, that the mystical bond and gift of working with horses has been a constant thread inexplicably entwined throughout his life.

After over 35 years of research into horse training, psychology and Human personal growth & development, Robert: Author, Trainer, Farrier, Teacher, would like to take this opportunity to share with you his insight into his innovative approach to teaching horses and ourselves.

This could be the dawn of a new experience and the promise of a powerful journey of spiritual growth for both you and your horse.

He calls it The Cornerstone Approach.

He is available to hold symposiums around the world.

E-mail: info@cornerstoneapproach.ca

http://www.cornerstoneapproach.ca

http://www.robertmclardie.com

BOOKS WEB-SITE URL IS:
http://www.theoldmanwisdom.com

A WAY TO HIGHER LEARNING

The more I think I know,

The more I realise how little I know,

Then truly I am free to start to learn.

I have to first learn to reduce my ego, my pride and arrogance.

Do you remember what it was to be "Child Like?"

To wonder at it all.

To ask questions, to want to know, to learn.

To understand truly.

That at times is what we have to return to.

Become "Child Like."

And in "Child Like Innocence" – Becoming fully aware.

Free to move onto a higher level of learning.

Being this free, will allow you to use your imagination,

What you so often create in your imagination,

Happens in your life or riding.

It's a never ending journey of growth and renewal.

Stay green and in "Child Like" awe, keep growing

To a higher level of learning.

Robert J. McLardie

www.ingramcontent.com/pod-product-compliance
Lightning Source LLC
Chambersburg PA
CBHW021811220426
43662CB00006B/265